NEW TYPO GRAPHICS 2

P·I·E Books
Villa Phoenix Suite 301, 4-14-6 Komagome,
Toshima-ku, Tokyo 170 Japan Tel:03-3940-8302
Fax:03-3576-7361
e-mail: piebooks@bekkoame.or.jp

ISBN 4-89444-056-3 C3070 ¥15500E

First published in Germany 1997 by:
NIPPAN / Nippon Shuppan Hanbai Deutschland GmbH
Krefelder Straße 85, D-40549 Düsseldorf, Germany
Tel:0211-5048080/89 Fax:0211-5049326

ISBN 3-910052-94-0

Printed in Singapore

Contents

Typographie kann nur Text sein; sie kann aber auch ein Schlüsselelement eines stimulierenden Visuals sein. Oft experimentell ist Typographie eine Herausforderung in zwei Hinsichten. Einerseits ist eine Balance zu finden zwischen Lesbarkeit und ästhetischen Ansprüchen, andererseits sollen auch neue Stile, die kontinuierlich neu geschaffen werden, akzeptiert und berücksichtigt werden. In unserer modernen, zersplitterten Gesellschaft kann die Vielfalt des Designs nicht konfrontieren, sondern muß auf Koexistenz ausgelegt sein.
Dieses Buch möchte einen Überblick über den derzeitigen Status der Typographie geben. Es soll eine Ideenquelle für alle Designer sein, die mit Schrift arbeiten, wie auch ein wertvolles Referenzwerk zur Exploration der Möglichkeiten und Variationen der Typographie der Zukunft.
Fünf Designer, alle in völlig verschiedenen Bereichen arbeitend, haben uns für diese Einleitung von "New Typographics 2" ihre Gedanken über Typographie zur Verfügung gestellt. Wir hoffen, daß diese Kommentare, zusammen mit den hier präsentierten Arbeiten, dem Leser ein Gefühl für die heute real existierende Welt der Typographie geben.

Die Diversifikation der Typographie

多様化するタイポグラフィ

テキストとしてのタイポグラフィ、刺激的なビジュアルの一部としてのタイポグラフィ、実験的なタイポグラフィ、文字の可読性への挑戦と美的追求、そして、常に存在する新しいものへの寛容と、あらゆるスタイルの融合… 現在のセグメント化された社会では、デザインの多様性もまた、対立するのではなく共存していくはずです。様々なタイポグラフィが共存している現在の状況を一望できる本書は、文字を扱うすべてのクリエイターにとって創作のヒントとなり、タイポグラフィの今後の可能性と多様性を探る良い資料となるはずです。今回は「ニュータイポグラフィックス2」のイントロダクションとして、まったく異なるフィールドで活躍する5人のデザイナーの方にコメントを寄せていただきました。本書掲載の作品と合わせて、現在の "タイポ" を感じていただけたらと思います。

Vorwort
イントロダクション
Introduction

The Diversification of Typography

Typography can be text; it can be a key part of a stimulating visual. Often experimental, typography provides a challenge in balancing readability with more aesthetic objectives, as well as demanding tolerance in acceptance of the new styles that are continually being created. In today's segmented society, the diversity of designs cannot conflict but must be able to co-exist.
This book aims to present an overview of the current state of typography. It should be a source of ideas for all designers who work with type, as well as a valuable reference for exploring the possibilities and variations of typography's future.
For the following introduction to "New Typographics 2," five designers, all working in completely different fields, have provided us with their thoughts regarding typography. We hope that their comments, along with the works presented in this book, will give the reader a sense of the world of typography that exists today.

Liisa Salonen リーサ・サローネン

InFlux

Derzeitige Typography ist eine fliessende Geste. Das kontinuierliche Spiel und Wiederholungsspiel der Informationen in dem Spektakel der zeitgenössischen Kultur erfordert liquide Flexibilität. Und die Mutationen in digitaler Typographie reflektieren den fundamentalen Wandel vom Papier zum Bildschirm, von Permanenz zur Aufführung. Für mich ist die Akrobatik der aktuellen Typographie ein karnevalistisches Idiom. Seit dem Mittelalter an die populäre Kultur gebunden, werden heute karnevalistische Formen revitalisiert in Raves und in der Kunst des "neuen" Zirkus, im multiplen Bodypiercing und in Tattoos. Charakterisiert durch einen starken Sinn von Wandel und Erneuerung ist das eine Sprache von Respektlosigkeit und Revolte. Die spielerischen, undefinierten und verbundenen Formen werden einer spiessigen Seriosität, zu Autorität, zu fix-fertigen Lösungen, zu Vorhersehbarkeit entgegengesetzt. [1]

Wiedergeboren auf dem Bildschirm als Licht via Computer-Code, werden die alten Fonts erneuert in endlosen Maskeraden und Verzerrungen. Animation, Flux und Metamorphose sind Charakteristika, die in Fonts hineingelegt werden und in ihre Anwendungen in digitalen Videos und interaktiven Applikationen. Ich beziehe mich auf transformative Fonts wie Walker (geschaffen von Matthew Carter für das Walker Art Center) mit seinen entfernbaren, anheftbaren Serifen und Detroit MM (gestaltet an der Cranbrook Academy of Art von Stefane Delgado, Gilles Gavillet und David Rust), einem Muliple-Master-Font mit variablen Laufweiten und Kurven. Diese Fonts repräsentieren die breitere kulturelle Erscheinung einer fluiden Typographie, die fähig ist, über ihre historischen Limitationen hinauszugehen.

[1] Bakhtin, Mikhail: *Rabelais and his World.*
Bloomington, Indiana. Indiana University Press, 1984. Seite 3

Profil: **Liisa Salonen**
Ausgewandert nach Amerika und jetzt in Kanada lebend, hat Liisa Salonen 1997 an der Cranbrook Academy of Arts ihr Diplom gemacht. Zuletzt hat sie an Words+Pictures für Business+Culture gearbeitet. Ihre Arbeiten wurden publiziert und ausgestellt in USA, Kanada, England und Polen.

インフラックス

現代のタイポグラフィは流動的なジェスチャーである。現代カルチャーのスペクタクルの中で、絶え間ない情報のプレイとリプレイは液体のように流動的な形状を必要とする。デジタル・タイポグラフィへの変遷は、紙からスクリーンへ、固定性からパフォーマンスへと根本的な移行を反映している。今日のタイポグラフィが演じる芸は『カーニバル的』である。中世からポップ・カルチャーと密接な関係にあった『カーニバル的なもの』は、今日も、パーティや新サーカスやボディ・ピアシングそしてタトゥーに生命を与えた。カーニバルとは、変化とリニューアルという強い感覚的特徴を持つ、不適切と反抗の言語である。その遊びに満ちた、定義のない、組み換え型のフォルムは、狭量な生真面目さや権威主義や用意された解決や予測可能性とは相反するものである。[1]

コンピューターのコードによって光のごとくスクリーン上に生まれ変わり、古いフォントは、終わりのない仮面舞踊会や曲芸を通してリニューアルされた。アニメーション、流動、変化(へんげ)がフォントのデザインにおける特徴であり、それらがデジタルのスクリーンやインタラクティブなアプリケーションの中でパフォーマンスをする。これは、例えばWalker(マシュー・カーターのデザインによるウォーカー・アートセンターのためのフォント)に見られる、取り外し可能なスナップ方式のセリフ(ひげ飾り部分)や、デトロイトMMに見られる(ステファン・デルガド、ジル・ガビレ、デイビッド・ラストによってクランブルック・アカデミー・オブ・アートにおいてデザインされた)さまざまな幅とカーブを備えたマスターフォントなどがそうである。これらの例は、流動的なフォントがより幅のある文化に対応することを示しており、過去の限界を超えて応用が可能である。

(1)『Rabelais and His World』3ページより。ミハイル・バフーチンの言葉。
1984年インディアナ大学出版、インディアナ州ブルーミントン。

プロフィール:**リーサ・サローネン**
カナダ在住アメリカ人。1997年クランブルック・アカデミー・オブ・アートを卒業、MFA取得。最近の仕事は、Words+Pictures for Business+Culture。作品はアメリカ、カナダ、イギリス、ポーランドで紹介されている。

InFlux

Current typography is a fluid gesture. The continuous play and replay of information in the spectacle of contemporary culture demands a liquid flexibility. And the mutations in digital typography reflect a fundamental shifting from paper to screen, from permanence to performance. For me, the acrobatics of today's typography express a carnivalesque idiom. Tied to popular culture since medieval times, carnival forms are revitalized in raves and in the art of the "new" circus, in multiple body piercings and tattoos. Characterized by a strong sense of change and renewal, it is a language of irreverence and revolt. The playful, undefined and recombinant forms are opposed to all narrow-minded seriousness, to authoritarianism, to ready-made solutions, to predictability. [1]

Reborn on the screen as light via computer code, the old fonts are renewed in endless masquerades and contortions. Animation, flux and metamorphosis are characteristics designed into fonts and their performance in digital video and interactive applications. I'm referring to transformative fonts such as Walker (designed by Matthew Carter for the Walker Art Center), with its removable, snap-on serifs, and DetroitMM (designed at Cranbrook Academy of Art by Stefane Delgado, Gilles Gavillet and David Rust), a multiple master font with variable widths and curves. These fonts represent the broader cultural appearance of a fluid typography capable of extending beyond its historical limitations.

[1] Bakhtin, Mikhail. *Rabelais and His World.*
(Bloomington, Indiana: Indiana University Press, 1984], 3,11.

Profile: **Liisa Salonen**
An expatriate American living in Canada, she completed an MFA at Cranbrook Academy of Art in 1997. She has worked most recently at Words+Pictures for Business+Culture, and her work has been published and exhibited in the United States, Canada, the United Kingdom and Poland.

Rian Hughes リアン・ヒューズ

Friede der Typographie

Ich unterscheide nicht zwischen Typographie und Illustration, zwischen Illustration und Graphik-Design: ihnen liegen die gleichen ästhetischen Ansprüche zugrunde. Trotzdem erscheint die Schrift von allen das beste Werkzeug, um damit die subatomaren Realitäten von Form und Gestalt zu demonstrieren - gleichsam wie ein Physiker im Laboratorium des Visuellen. Die Eigenschaften von Kurve und Linie, vertikal und horizontal sind immer noch die wichtigsten Elemente, die in den großen Maßstäben des realen Lebens eine spezifische Atmosphäre vermitteln können. Diese kann von einem futuristischen zwanzigjährigen TV Optimismus zu einem altmodischen, angebrochenen Kunststoff-Warnschild in der Pariser Metro reichen. Diese Bemerkungen sind nur ein Anfangspunkt: Ein Font steht auch anderen Designern zur Verfügung, und der Gebrauch (wie auch Missbrauch), den er erfährt, nachdem er seinen Schöpfer verlassen hat, wird auf eine nicht vorsehbare Weise seine Ausstrahlung formen. Schrift entwickelt sich, nachdem sie dem Labor entsprungen ist, und die stärksten virulenten Charaktere haben ein Eigenleben. Sie sind es, die letztentlich den Zeitgeist artikulieren.

Profil: **Rian Hughes und Device**
Rian Hughes und Device bieten Schrift, Design und Illustration als Service für Werbekampagnen, Schallplatten-/CD-Cover, Buchumschläge, Buchillustrationen, Film- und TV-Titel. Auch werden auf Wunsch eigene Schriften entworfen. Fonts sind erhältlich unter (devicefonts.co.uk oder email: rianhughes@compuserve.com)

タイポグラフィの作品

タイポグラフィとイラストレーション、イラストレーションとグラフィックデザインのそれぞれの間には何ら境界はないと思っている。それらの底流には、等しく美的な関係がある。しかし、中でもタイポグラフィは、フォルムと形の原子レベルの世界を探索する、最も鋭利なツールのように思える。それはあたかもビジュアルという実験室での物理学者のようである。カーブとライン、縦と横といった要素がタイポグラフィの直接的な問題であり、それが現実のものとなったとき、特定の雰囲気を伝えるのである。その雰囲気とは、20年前のTVプログラムの現代に通用する楽観主義から、ひと昔前のパリのメトロの、薄汚れたビニール製警告看板までさまざまである。

これらの暗示はほんの出発点に過ぎない。ひとつのフォントは、デザイナーの手を離れ、他人も使用できるようになる。その後は、受け取られ方によって異なった意味を持ちながら使用（そして誤用）されていく。どんな意味を持つのかは予測不可能である。タイポグラフィは、実験室を離れた後も進化していく。時代精神を反映するようになるほど強い種のフォントは、自ら生命を持つのである。

プロフィール：リアン・ヒューズ／ディバイス
リアン・ヒューズとディバイスは、タイポグラフィを始め、デザイン、イラストレーションのサービスを行っている。広告キャンペーン、レコード／CDカバー、ブックデザイン、グラフィック小説、映画やTVのタイトルやカスタムメイドのフォントのデザインまでその分野は多岐にわたる。フォントは自社レーベルによってリリースされている。
問い合せ；devicefonts.co.uk　または、rianhughes@compuserve.com

Piece on Typography

I recognize no division between typography and illustration, illustration and graphic design; the same aesthetic concerns underlie them all. However, of them all, type design seems the sharpest tool with which to probe the subatomic realms of form and shape like some physicist in the laboratory of the visual. The essentials of curve and line, vertical and horizontal, are upfront immediate concerns that still, on larger real-life scales, can convey a specific atmosphere that can range from a futuristic twenty-year-old TV optimism to yesterday's cracked Paris Metro vinyl warning sign. These connotations are merely a starting point: a font is available to other designers, and the usage (and abusage) it gets after it leaves its creator will shape its perceived meaning in ways that are impossible to foresee. Type evolves after escaping the design laboratory, and the most virulent strains that end up articulating the zeitgeist have a life all their own.

Profile: **Rian Hughes/Device**
Rian Hughes and Device provide type, design and illustration services for advertising campaigns, record/CD sleeves, book jackets, graphic novels, film and television titles, and custom font design. Fonts are released via their own label (devicefonts.co.uk or, email: rianhughes@compuserve.com).

Koeweiden Postma Associates
クーワイドゥン・ポストマ・アソシエイツ

Zwischen Türen

Über Design und Typographie zu schreiben ist nicht möglich, ohne den Inhalt des Prozesses anzusprechen. Wir hängen keiner Theorie an; wir haben keine Leitlinien, nach denen wir arbeiten; wir bieten auch kein "Manifest" oder "Firmengrundsätze", unter die unsere Arbeit eingeordnet werden kann. Unsere Methode ist mehr eine Kombination eines Gefühls im Bauch mit unseren ästhetischen Reaktionen auf das jeweilige Subjekt.

Erfolgreiche und innovative Typographie ist diskutierbarerweise das Resultat von etwas mehr als der Kenntnis der Regeln darüber, was in ist und neu. Intuition ist für uns ein nicht fassbarer Faktor, der ein Stück Typo/Design "gut" oder "richtig" macht. Wo ein Stück Design die Stufe erreicht hat, auf der es arbeitet, scheint die Intuition die extra Zutat zu sein, die es erinnerbar macht oder speziell. Ein Bild spricht tausend Worte, aber wie umgekehrt? Für uns ist der emotionale Wert, den die Typographie einem Wort geben kann, verbunden damit, dem Wort eine zusätzliche Schicht von Informationen zu geben, die das Wort alleine nicht erzielen kann. Wir streben immer an, Schrift und Bild auf eine Weise zu integrieren, die nicht nur ästhetisch gefallend sondern auch emotional komplett ist.

Bei unserer Arbeit geht es mehr um das Feeling als um Aussagen; aber wenn es eine verborgene Botschaft in unserer Arbeit gibt, dann ist es wahrscheinlich die Furcht, zu ernst genommen zu werden.

Wie mit jedem Designer, der bereit ist, nach innen zu schauen und seine Wurzeln und Einflüsse zu erkennen, bleiben wir in der Schuld der Leute, die uns inspiriert und gelehrt haben. Wir möchten deshalb Saul Bass, Paul Rand, Pierre Bernard, Gert Dumbar und vielen anderen danken.

Wenn wir darüber nachdenken, was uns antreibt, kann man sagen, daß unsere Arbeit genausoviel über das geht, was wir wissen, wie über das, was wir nicht wissen. Oder wie es der Sänger Jim Morrisson einst gesagt hat: "Da gibt es Dinge, die man kennt, und Dinge, die unbekannt sind. Und dazwischen sind Türen."

Studio-Profil: **Koeweiden Postma Associates**
Gegründet und ansässig in Amsterdam von Jacques Koeweiden und Paul Postma 1987. Koeweiden Postma Associates sind Jacques Koeweiden (CD), Paul Postma (CD), Dick de Groot (MD), Anneke Krull (D) & Ralf Schroeder (D). Obwohl der Schwerpunkt unserer Arbeit im Design liegt, arbeiten wir seit 1990 verstärkt in der, wie man so sagt, breiten Spanne zwischen Werbung und Design. Koeweiden Postma Associates arbeite(te) für Kunden wie Glaxso, Nickelodeon, Oilily, Nike, McDonalds, Heineken, Holländisches Aussenministerium, Randstad und kürzlich Canal+. Koeweiden Postma Associates erhielt zahlreiche Auszeichnungen, sowohl national wie international, u.a. vom ADC Holland, dem British D&AD, dem New York ADC, der British TIA, der The 100 Show. 1996 wurde Koeweiden Postma Associates von Graphis als eine der zehn besten Design-Agenturen gewählt.

扉の間で

プロセスの説明を省いては、デザインとタイポグラフィについて語ることはできない。私たちは、理論には固執していない。何らかのガイドラインにそって仕事をするわけでもない。クーワイドゥン・ポストマ・アソシエイツの作品の分類をもとに『声明』や『宣言』を発表するわけではない。むしろ、我々のやり方は直感と与えられた課題への美的なリアクションとの統合なのである。

イノベイティブで完成度の高いタイポグラフィは、明らかにルールや何が新しいかという知識以上のものの結果である。我々にとっては直感こそが、そのタイポやデザインの善し悪しを決める無形の要因である。一点のデザインが用途を満たす段階に達しているとしたら、それを記憶に残すような、あるいは特別なレベルに高めるための要因は直感なのである。

一枚の絵は何千という言葉を語る。だが、その逆はどうか。我々にとって、タイポグラフィとは、言葉に新たな情報の層を与えることによって、言葉にエモーショナルな価値を添えることである。それは、言葉そのものだけでは、到達し得ない。我々は常に、美的に優れているだけでなく、エモーショナルに完成されたタイポとイメージとの統合をめざしているのである。

我々の仕事は、声明ではなく、フィーリングであると述べたが、隠された声明があるとしたら、それは、あまりにもシリアスに受け取られることへの恐れ、かもしれない。

我々がデザインワークの中で影響を受けたり、ルーツとしていたり、内にその存在を認めるデザイナーがいる。ソール・バス、ポール・ランド、ピエール・ベルナール、ゲルト・ドゥンバー、その他多くの人々から受けた教えとインスパイアに謝辞を述べたい。

我々を駆り立てているものを考えてみると、我々の仕事には、我々が知っていることと同じくらい知らないことがあることであるといえる。あるいは、ジム・モリソンの言葉『世の中には知られていることと、知られていないことがある。その両者の間にはドアがある』である。

オフィスプロフィール: **クーワイドゥン・ポストマ・アソシエイツ**
1987年ジャック・クーワイドゥン、ポール・ポストマの二人によってアムステルダムで設立される。現在、クリエイティブ・ディレクターの2人の他、マネージング・ディレクターのディック・ドゥ・グロート、デザイナーのアネカ・クレル、ラルフ・シュルーダルから成る。デザインが主な仕事ではあるが、1990年より、いわゆる『広告とデザインとの大きな溝』を埋めようと仕事を続けている。クライアントおよび作品には、グラクソ、ニッケルオデオン、オイリリー、ナイキ、マクドナルド、ハイネケン、オランダ経済省、ランドスタットなどの企業広告、および最近ではフランスのケーブルTVネットワーク、カナル・プラスのTVグラフィックなどがある。また、国内外の数々の賞を受賞しており、オランダADC、イギリスD&AD、ニューヨークADC、ニューヨークTDC、イギリスTIA、The 100 Showなどがある。1996年にはグラフィスのデザイン会社トップ10のひとつに選ばれている。

Between Doors

Writing about design and typography is quite impossible without mentioning the content of the process. We do not adhere to a theory; we have no guidelines by which we work; we also don't offer a 'manifesto' or a 'corporate statement' under which our work can be classified. Rather, our method is an integration of gut feeling and our aesthetic reaction to the subject matter.

Successful and innovative typography is arguably the result of something more than a knowledge of the 'rules' of what's edgy & new. For us intuition is an intangible factor which makes a piece of type/design 'good' or 'right'. Where a piece of design has reached the stage where it works, intuition seems to be the extra ingredient which makes it become memorable or special.

A picture tells a thousand words, but how about the other way around? For us, the emotional value that typography can impart to a word has to do with giving the word an extra layer of information which the word alone cannot achieve. We always aim to integrate type and imagery in a way that is not only aesthetically pleasing, but emotionally complete as well.

Our work is more about feeling than statement but if there *is* a hidden statement in our work, it's probably the fear of being taken too seriously.

As with any designer who is prepared to look within and acknowledge his roots & influences, we remain indebted to those people who have inspired and taught us. We would therefore like to thank Saul Bass, Paul Rand, Pierre Bernard, Gert Dumber, and many others.

When reflecting upon what drives us, you could say that our work is as much about what we know as what we don't know. Or, as singer Jim Morrison put it once, 'There are things that are known and things that are unknown. And between them are doors.'

Office profile: **Koeweiden Postma Associates**
Formed and based in Amsterdam by Jacques Koeweiden and Paul Postma in 1987, Koeweiden Postma Associates are Jacques Koeweiden (CD), Paul Postma (CD), Dick de Groot (MD), Anneke Krull (D), and Ralf Schroeder (D). Although the main focus of their work is design, since 1990 they have been increasingly operating in what is considered the wide gap between advertising and design. The company works for international corporate and cultural clients, including Glaxo, Nickelodeon, Oilily, Nike, McDonald's, Heineken, the Dutch Ministry of Economic Affairs, Randstad, and Canal+. They have received much international recognition, including awards from the ADC Holland, the British D&AD, the New York ADC, the New York TDC, the British TIA, and The 100 Show. In 1996 they were chosen as one of the Graphis Ten Best Design Agencies.

Ralph Schraivogel
ラルフ・シュライフォーゲル

Und es ist doch ein Bild

Nirgends wird die Coexistenz von Bild und Typographie so unausweichlich zu einem zentralen Thema wie bei der Plakatgestaltung. Dies gilt sogar bei rein typografischen Lösungen. Auch ein Typoplakat wird zuerst als Bild wahrgenommen bevor es gelesen werden kann.

Ausnahmen stellen lediglich die sehr spärlich vorkommenden Plakate dar, die gänzlich ohne Text auskommen.

Jedes Bild stellt andere Bedingungen an die Typografie, - lässt jenes zu, - schliesst anderes aus, und umgekehrt.

Auch das Manuskript, welches meistens als Erstes schon in definitivier Form vorliegt, stellt gewisse Bedingungen durch den Umfang, den Inhalt und die Struktur, Weshalb es naheliegend ist, schon zu Beginn des Entwurfprozesses auch typografische Untersuchungen anzustellen.

Denn die Typografie ist, unabhängig davon, ob ihr im Plakat eine dominierende oder eine untergeordnete Rolle zugesprochen wird, im gleichen Mass unerbittlich und kennt keine Gnade.

Bild und Text müssen sich, gleichzeitig auf einer in einem Blick erfassbaren Fläche, optimal ergänzen. Diese Anforderung ist dermassen komplex, dass typografische Dogmen zu kurz greifen und schlichtweg unbrauchbar sind. Die Beziehung Bild - Typografie oder Tyopgrafie - Bild muss von Fall zu Fall neu, in all seinen Facetten, untersucht werden.

Das Plakat wird zuerst, in seiner gesamten Erscheinung inklusiv der Typografie, als Bild wahrgenommen. Auch für ein Plakat ist der erste Eindruck entscheidend. Die Grenzen zwischen Bild und Typografie werden somit, ob wir wollen oder nicht, spätestens vom Betrachter aufgelöst.

Profil: **Ralph Schraivogel AGI**
Seit 1982, nach Beendigung der Ausbildung, betreibe ich ein Designstudio. Mein Studio verstehe ich nicht als Dienstleistungsbetrieb. Den Auftrag betrachte ich als Anlass für meine Bildarbeit. Mein Hauptbetätigungsfeld ist die Plakatgestaltung. Die Auftraggeber sind Museen, Kinos, Theater, Filmemacher, Schriftsteller, Musiker...
Seit 1992 bin ich Dozent an der Schule für Gestaltung Zürich.

すべてはイメージとして

ポスターデザインほど、イメージとタイポグラフィの共存が不可避的に主なテーマになっているものはない。そして、このテーマは、純粋なタイポグラフィの融合にも有効である。タイポグラフィ中心のポスターは、読まれるより先にイメージとして捉えられる。例外はごくまれで、テキストのないデザインのみである。個々のイメージが、それぞれのタイポグラフィに異なる役割を与える。イメージはタイポグラフィの存在を許可したり、排除したり、またはその逆もあり得る。

テキストもまた、最初に決まった形で提出されるが、全体の長さ、内容、および構造によってある種の束縛を持つ。そのため、デザインプロセスのごく初期の段階でタイポグラフィとしてのリサーチを行うことが実際的である。タイポグラフィはポスターにおいて支配的にも準支配的にもなり得る。タイポグラフィはどれもみな、有無を言わさず獰猛である。

イメージとテキストは、与えられたスペースの中で、最良に溶け合うものでなくてはならない。これは、非常に複雑な仕事であり、そのためにタイポグラフィの定則をはずれたり、完全に非実用的なものになったりする。イメージ-タイポグラフィ、タイポグラフィ-イメージ間の関係は、個々のケースについてあらゆる側面でゼロから分析されなければならない。

ポスターはタイポグラフィを含めてトータルなイメージとして受け取られる。最初の印象ですべて決まるのである。

イメージとタイポグラフィの境界は、我々が望むと望まないとに関わらず、最終的には観る者によって溶け合うのである。

プロフィール：ラルフ・シュライフォーゲル AGI
1982年卒業後、デザインスタジオを主宰。自身のスタジオはサービス会社ではなく、ひとつひとつの仕事が自身のアーティスティックなイメージワークであると考えている。最も興味があり、かつ専門としているのはポスターデザインである。クライアントは、美術館、映画館、劇場、映画監督、作家、ミュージシャンなどである。1992年以来、チューリッヒの造形学校において講義を担当している。

In Spite of All It Is Still a Picture

Nowhere else more than in poster design does the coexistence of image and typography inevitably become a central topic. A typo-poster is recognized as an image before it is read. Exceptions are those very few posters which are produced without text at all. Each image gives typography a specific task, allows or excludes it, and vice-versa.

The copy itself, which normally must be used in a definitive form, creates certain restraints because of its length, content, and structure. It is therefore practical to undertake typographic research at the very beginning of the design process. Typography may have the dominant or subdominant role in a poster; typography can be extremely powerful.

Image and text need to merge optimally in a space to be recognized at one glance. This task is highly complex, and typographic dogma becomes irrelevant and totally useless. All facets of the relationship – typography/image, or image/typography – need to be analyzed from scratch in each individual case.

The poster in its totality, inclusive of type, is at first perceived as one image. For a poster, the first impression is decisive.

The borders between Image and Type are dissolved from the viewer at last, whether we want them to be or not.

Profile: **Ralph Schraivogel, AGI**
After finishing studies in 1982, established his own independent design studio. "I do not see my studio as a service bureau. Each assignment is a reason for my artistic image work. Of particular interest to me, and my specialty, is poster design. I get jobs from museums, cinemas, theaters, movie directors, authors, musicians..."
Since 1992, he has been a lecturer at the Schule für Gestaltung, Zürich, Switzerland.

Phunk Studio / Guerilla Fonts
パンクスタジオ／ゲリラフォンツ

Visuelle Junkies

"Visuelle Junkies" - diesen Spitznamen haben wir uns selbst gegeben. Wir haben uns der visuellen Bilderwelt verschrieben, die ständig unsere Sinne bombardiert. Seien es MTV, Filme, Comics, Schallplattenhüllen oder die letzte Ausgabe von Emigre. Wir geniessen sie mit Freude... hungrig nach mehr... Dann kommt der kreative Prozess, Verdauung der verschiedenen Einflüsse... die dann übersetzt werden in unsere Arbeiten. Beispiele der verschiedenen visuellen Elemente kann man an allen unseren Werken erkennen. Wir sehen die letzte Truppe der Typographen wie uns ähnlich den Burschen, die Schlagzeug-Maschinen und Mixer annehmen, um elektronische Musik zu produzieren. In unserem Falle ist dies der Mac. Die Fonts, die wir herstellen, werden nicht mehr in Metall gegossen. Sehr ähnlich den Chemical Brothers, die auch kein tradionelles Instrument mehr spielen. Ob die neue Welle der elektronischen Schriftgestalter Codes für die Zukunft der Kommunikation produzieren, ist offen für Interpretation. Wir glauben, daß die Kenntnis der Typographie und ihrer Regeln unabdingbar ist für die Kreation guter typographischer Arbeiten. Typographie ist eine visuelle Sprache, wie jede andere Sprache, die sich andauernd entwickelt, beeinflusst von Technologie und Kultur. Singapore ist eine multi-kulturelle Gesellschaft, die keine Design-Tradition hat, nur einen eigenen Dialekt der visuellen Sprache. Das ist für uns eine befreiende Chance zu experimentieren und mit diesem eigenen Dialekt zu sprechen.

Studio-Profil: **Phunk Studio/Guerilla Fonts**
Gegründet im Dezember 1994 von Jackson Tan Tzun Tat, William Chan Wai Liam und Alvin Tan Boon Sing, nachdem sie das Lasalle College für Kunst in Singapore abgeschlossen hatten. Gründeten vor kurzem Guerilla Fonts, um auch nicht selbst gestaltete Schriften zu vertreiben. Zur Zeit dabei, eine unabhängiges Graphik-Design-Zeitschrift in Singapore zu etablieren. Einige ihrer Fonts werden zur Zeit von Garage Fonts, Del Mar, Californien, vertrieben. Arbeiten kann man sehen unter http://home.pacific.net.sg/~zero1.

ビジュアル・ジャンキー

『ビジュアル・ジャンキース』自分たちのことをこう呼んでいる。私たちの感覚に絶えず砲撃を仕掛けてくるビジュアルのイメージに病みつきになってしまった。それらは、MTVや映画、コミック、アルバム・カバーであったり、エミグレの最新版であったりする。私たちは喜んでそれらをむさぼり食う…もっと、もっと、貪欲に…。そして、クリエイティブなプロセスに移る。さまざまな影響を受けたものが消化され、それらは作品に吸収されていく。私たちの作品には、さまざまなビジュアルのサンプリングが見られる。私たちのような新しいタイポグラファーは、ドラムとミキサーを使ってエレクトロニック・ミュージックを生み出す"バンド"のようである。私たちの場合の道具はMacである。私たちが創るフォントはもはや活版用の鉄の鋳型ではないし、どんな型にもはまらない。楽器を演奏できないケミカル・ブラザーズのようである。エレクトロニックなタイポグラファーたちが、未来のコミュニケーションの鍵となるものを生みだせるかどうかはわからない。だが、私たちは、タイポグラフィとそのルールについて知ることは、良い作品を創る上で不可欠であると考えている。タイポグラフィはビジュアルの言語であり、他のさまざまな言語同様、テクノロジーや文化の影響を受けて絶え間なく進化している。シンガポールはデザインの伝統がなく、ビジュアル言語のスラングを持たない多文化の社会である。私たちにとってこれはデザインの探訪であり、独自のスラングで話し始めるためのチャンスなのである。

オフィスプロフィール：パンクスタジオ／ゲリラフォンツ
1994年12月、シンガポールのラサール・カレッジ・オブ・アートを卒業したジャクソン・タン、ウィリアム・チャンとアルビン・タンによって設立される。最近になって、自身のデザインしたフォントを販売するためゲリラ・フォンツを設立。現在は、シンガポールでグラフィック・デザインのインディペンデント雑誌をスタートさせようと取り組んでいる。何種かのフォントは、カリフォルニア州のデル・マーにあるガレージ・フォンツによって販売されている。
作品をご覧になりたい場合は、http://home.pacific.net.sg/~zero1

Visual Junkies

'Visual Junkies' - a nickname that we call ourselves. We are hooked on visual imageries constantly bombarding our senses. Be it MTV, films, comics, album covers, or the latest copy of Emigre. We devour them with delight... hungry for more... Then comes the creative process, digestion of the various influences... which are then translated into our works. Sampling of various visual elements can be seen throughout our works. We see the latest band of typographers like us similar to the guys picking up drum machines and mixers to produce electronic music. In our case it is the Mac. The fonts that we produce are no longer cast in metal. Much like the Chemical Brothers do not play any traditional instruments themselves. Whether the new wave of electronic type designers are producing codes for the future of communications is open to interpretations. We do believe that knowledge of typography and its rules are essential to the creation of good typographic works. Typography is a visual language; like any other languages, it is constantly evolving, influenced by technology and culture. Singapore is a multi-cultural society that does not have a design tradition or its own slang of the visual language. It is a liberating chance for us to explore and to speak with our own slang of the visual language.

Office Profile: **Phunk Studio / Guerilla Fonts**
Formed in Dec. 1994 by Jackson Tan Tzun Tat, William Chan Wai Liam, and Alvin Tan Boon Siang after they graduated from Lasalle College of the Art in Singapore. Started Guerilla Fonts recently to distribute fonts that they have designed. Currently working on starting an independent Graphic Design magazine in Singapore. Some of their fonts are currently distributed by Garage Fonts. Del Mar. California. Works can be seen at http://home.pacific.net.sg/~zero1

Editorial Notes

Credit Format クレジットフォーマット

Title of artwork　タイトル
Country from which submitted　国名
Year of completion　制作年
Item　アイテム
Creative staff　制作スタッフ
CD:Creative director
AD:Art director
D: Designer
P: Photographer
I: Illustrator
CW:Copywriter
PD:Producer
DF:Design firm
A: Agency
CL:Client
Principal typeface　タイプフェイス

提供者の意向により、クレジットデータの一部に掲載していないものがあります。

Please note that some credit data has been omitted at the request of the submittor.

Archigram 1961-74
(Architecture and Performance)

Switzerland 1995 Poster ポスター
D: Ralph Schraivogel
Printer: Serigraphie Uldry
DF: R. Schraivogel Design
CL: Zürich Museum of Design
• House made,
  Berlin Grotesk Upright Medium

1. *Solothurn Literature Days*

Switzerland 1996 Poster ポスター
D: Ralph Schraivogel
Printer: Serigraphie Uldry
DF: R. Schraivogel Design
CL: Solothurner Literaturtage
• Typewriter + Fax

2. *The World in the Box - From the Camera Obscura to Audiovision*

Switzerland 1994 Poster ポスター
D: Ralph Schraivogel
Printer: Serigraphie Uldry
DF: R. Schraivogel Design
CL: Museum Strauhof
• Neuzeit S Bold,
 Neuzeit-Grotesk Bold Condensed

3. *Tala Mudra Rasa*

Switzerland 1996 Poster ポスター
D: Ralph Schraivogel
Printer: Serigraphie Uldry
DF: R. Schraivogel Design
CL: Zürich Museum of Design
• Quorum

Mainartery Calendar Poster 1996

UK 1995 Calendar カレンダー
CD: Jo Mirowski
AD: Peter Hayward
D: Scott Minshal
DF, CL: Mainartery Design

1. *Autonoma Solidaria*

Spain Poster ポスター
CD, D: Lluis Jubert
AD, D: Ramon Enrich
P: Ramon Pallarés
CW, DF: Espai Grafic
CL: Universitat Autonoma de Barcelona
• Barmeno, Sintax

2. *Cartell SAF*

Spain Poster ポスター
CD, D: Lluis Jubert
AD, D: Ramon Enrich
CW, DF: Espai Grafic
CL: Universitat Autonoma de Barcelona
• Futura, Officina

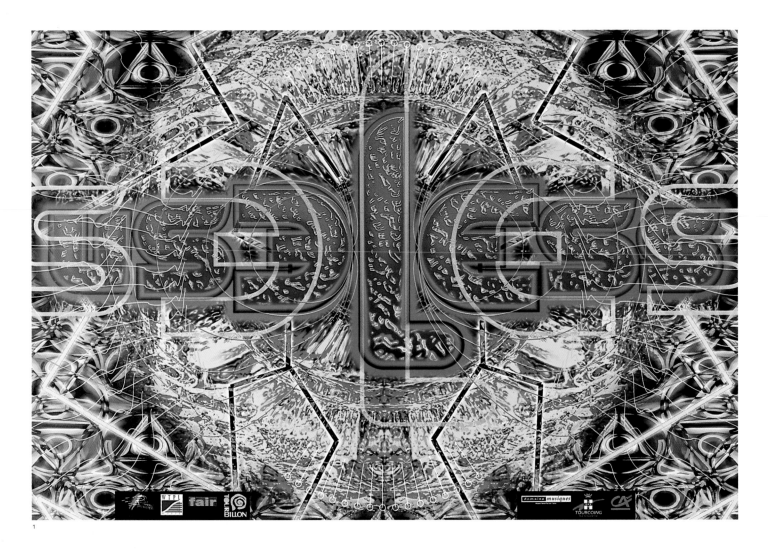

1

2

1. **Useless**

France 1996 Poster ポスター
CD, AD, D: Jean-Jacques Tachdjian
DF: i comme image
CL: Tourbilion
• Centauri [Radiateur® Fontes]

2. **Marc M**

France 1996 Poster ポスター
CD, AD, D: Jean-Jacques Tachdjian
DF: i comme image
CL: Easy Dub Ducasse
• Diner [Radiateur® Fontes]

1. *Hast du die Grossmutter schon besucht???*

Switzerland 1996 Poster ポスター
D: MBrunner
DF: Büro Destruct
CL: Kleintheater Freiburg
• Trade Gothic

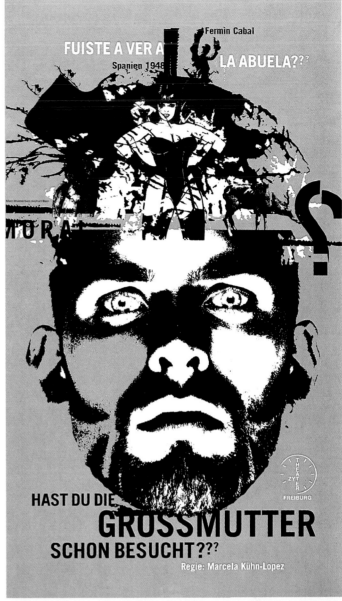

2. *Alien Parti*

France 1996 Poster ポスター
CD, AD, D: Jean-Jacques Tachdjian
DF: i comme image
CL: Nostromo Production
• Handmade + Radiateur® Fontes

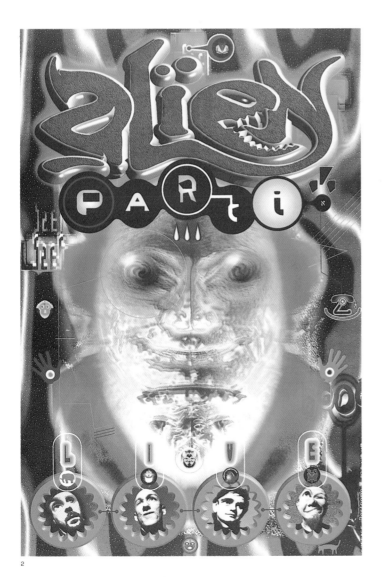

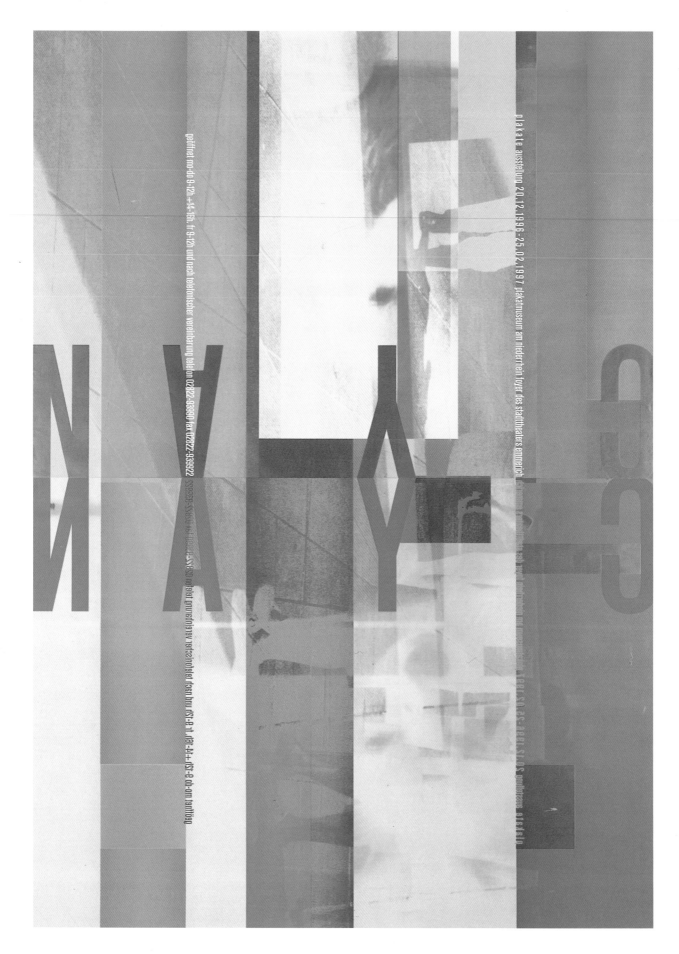

Cyan, Plakate

Germany 1996 Poster ポスター
D: Daniela Haufe / Sophie Alex
　/ Detlef Fiedler
CW, DF: Cyan
CL: Plakatmuseum Niedurrhein
• Univers

1. *Lichtraume*

Germany 1994 Poster ポスター
D: Daniela Haufe / Sophie Alex
/ Detlef Fiedler
CW, DF: Cyan
CL: Bauhaus Dessau Foundation

2. *Programme Posters - kunst in parochial*

Germany 1994 Poster ポスター
D: Daniela Haufe / Sophie Alex
/ Detlef Fiedler
CW, DF: Cyan
CL: Parochial-Kirche Berlin
• Garamond Amsterdam

Programme Poster - March

Germany 1996 Poster ポスター
D: Daniela Haufe / Sophie Alex
/ Detlef Fiedler
CW, DF: Cyan
CL: Bauhaus Dessau Foundation
• Ad Grotesk

1

2

3

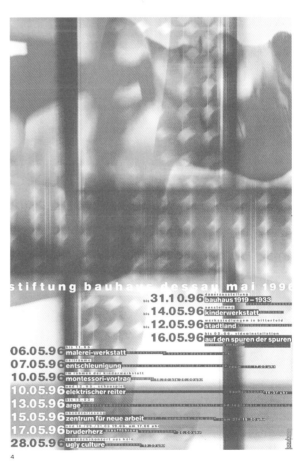

4

1. *Programme Poster - June*

Germany 1996 Poster ポスター
D: Daniela Haufe / Sophie Alex
 / Detlef Fiedler
CW, DF: Cyan
CL: Bauhaus Dessau Foundation
• Ad Grotesk

2. *Programme Poster - October*

Germany 1996 Poster ポスター
D: Daniela Haufe / Sophie Alex
 / Detlef Fiedler
CW, DF: Cyan
CL: Bauhaus Dessau Foundation
• Ad Grotesk

3. *Programme Poster - April*

Germany 1997 Poster ポスター
D: Daniela Haufe / Sophie Alex
 / Detlef Fiedler
CW, DF: Cyan
CL: Bauhaus Dessau Foundation
• Ad Grotesk

4. *Programme Poster - May*

Germany 1996 Poster ポスター
D: Daniela Haufe / Sophie Alex
 / Detlef Fiedler
CW, DF: Cyan
CL: Bauhaus Dessau Foundation
• Ad Grotesk

MONDAY, MAY 13, 1996
FRESH DIALOGUE {7:00 PM}
FASHION INSTITUTE OF TECHNOLOGY
Katie Murphy Amphitheatre
→227 WEST 27th STREET New York City

THE [ANNUAL MEETING] OF THE AIGA/NY CHAPTER WILL
BE HELD AT 6:30 P.M. IMMEDIATELY PRIOR TO FRESH DIALOGUE,
AND IS OPEN TO CHAPTER MEMBERS ONLY. ALL CHAPTER
Members are encouraged to attend and participate.

Admission:
AIGA/NY CHAPTER MEMBERS: $10.–
NON MEMBERS: $15.–
STUDENTS (WITH VALID ID): $5.–
F.I.T. STUDENTS ARE ADMITTED FREE OF CHARGE
AIGA/NEW YORK CHAPTER
164 FIFTH STREET NEW YORK, NY 10036

AIGA/NY CHAPTER EXECUTIVE COMMITTEE 1995–1996
PRESIDENT: KENNETH W. DOUBLEDAY
TREASURER: DENNIS BARNETT
SECRETARY: JIM ANDERSON
VICE PRESIDENTS: LAVINE SHIRARMAN
LYNDA DECKER, MARGERY GREENSPAN
J. GRAHAM HANSSON, CARLOS HEWITT
MARGIE LEVIN, ROBIN LYNCH, SETH PLATER-
DILLER, AMANDA WINDLEY
ADMINISTRATOR: LESLIE ADLER

THE MISSION OF THE NEW YORK CHAPTER OF THE
AMERICAN INSTITUTE OF GRAPHIC ARTS
(AIGA|NY) IS TO IDENTIFY AND DEFINE CRITICAL ISSUES
TO THE MEMBERSHIP AND THE GRAPHIC DESIGN
PROFESSION; TO EXPLORE AND CHANGE THOSE
ISSUES FOR THE PURPOSE OF HEIGHTENING THE STANDARDS OF GRAPHIC
DESIGN BUSINESS PRACTICE AND THE ART OF GRAPHIC DESIGN; TO CREATE
A FORUM FOR THE EXCHANGE OF INFORMATION, VIEWS, STYLE, AND TECHNIQUES AMONG
THOSE ENGAGED IN THE PROFESSION.
THE AIGA|NY GRATEFULLY ACKNOWLEDGES ITS PARTNERS IN DESIGN FOR THEIR SIGNIFICANT
CONTRIBUTIONS AND CONTINUING SUPPORT OF OUR EDUCATIONAL PROGRAMS:
NATIONAL REPROGRAPHICS INC., NEW YORK, NY; SPEED GRAPHICS, INC., NY, NY;
TYPOGRAM, INC., NEW YORK, NY;
PAMELA SYSTEM GRAPHICS; NEW YORK AND ST. PAUL.

FRESH DIALOGUE

→ LISA KROHN ←

IN INDUSTRIAL DESIGNER SINCE PERFECTING FROM ARCHITECT IN
A BROWN UNIVERSITY IN 1985, LISA KROHN WENT ON TO FINISH A MFA
PUBLICATIONS IN 1989. SHE FOUNDED KROHN DESIGN,
AT CRANBROOK IN 1988. AFTER WINNING THE GRAND PRIZE IN THE
FORMA FINLANDIA COMPETITION FOR HER LANDMARK AN INTERLINING CONCEPT,
SHE WENT TO MILAN AS A FELLOWSHIP TO WORK WITH MARIO BELLINI.
CURRENTLY PRACTICING IN ART CENTER,
AND TEACHING AT Art Center.
FOR A VARIETY OF DESIGN & ARCHITECTURE
SCI ARC AND CALARTS, KROHN ALSO WORKS
AGENCY-DISCIPLINARY STUDIO DESIGNING EVERYTHING
FROM CONSUMER GOODS TO A HYBRID POWERED
AUTOMOBILE. SHE STARTED KRAB DESIGN IN 1995
WHICH MANUFACTURES AND MARKETS FURNITURE
AND LIGHTING. HER WORK IS IN PERMANENT COLLECTIONS
THE MUSEUM OF MODERN ART,
THE Cooper-Hewitt NATIONAL
DESIGN MUSEUM,
THE CRANBROOK MUSEUM
AND THE DESIGN EXHIBIT
IN LONDON.

STEFAN SAGMEISTER

STEFAN SAGMEISTER, A NATIVE OF Austria, RECEIVED A MFA IN
GRAPHIC DESIGN FROM THE UNIVERSITY FOR APPLIED ARTS IN VIENNA
FOLLOWED BY A MASTERS IN COMMUNICATION DESIGN FROM Pratt INSTITUTE.
HE WAS AWARDED A FULBRIGHT GRANT IN 1986 AND SPENT HIS EARLY
CAREER EXPERIENCE BETWEEN NEW YORK AND VIENNA. SAGMEISTER
THEN SPENT TWO OF PERHAPS THE MOST FORMATIVE YEARS OF HIS CAREER
AS HEAD OF LEO BURNETT'S DESIGN GROUP IN HONG KONG.
THAT EXPERIENCE LED HIM BACK TO NEW YORK WHERE, AFTER
A STINT AT M&CO, HE FORMED SAGMEISTER INC. IN 1993.
BRANDISHING HIS MOTTO OF "STYLE = FART",
SAGMEISTER'S PRACTICE TODAY RANGES FROM
CORPORATE IDENTITIES TO CD COVERS FOR LOU REED,
DAVID BYRNE'S LUAKA BOP LABEL AND THE
GRAMMY NOMINATED CD PACKAGING DESIGN
"MOUNTAINS OF MADNESS."

/ io360 /

→ IN LESS THAN 2 YEARS, io360 HAS BUILT ONE OF
THE HOTTEST NEW MULTI-DISCIPLINARY DESIGN STUDIOS
WORKING IN A VARIETY OF MEDIA ENVIRONMENTS.
IO'S SQUARE BLENDS DISCIPLINES AND WIDE RANGING
AS CONTEMPORARY ARCHITECTURE AND
PROGRAMMING TO PROJECTS RANGING
FROM WEB SITES (JUST DEVELOPED FOR
PUBLIC INTERACTION GAMES SHOWN) TO
VIDEO GRAPHICS, CUSTOM INTERFACE DESIGN
AND CD-ROM DEVELOPMENT. THEY HAVE
BUILT A CLIENT LIST INCLUDING MAJOR
ENTERTAINMENT, PUBLISHING, ADVERTISING
AND TELECOMMUNICATIONS COMPANIES AS WELL
AS MUSEUMS AND EVEN AN ORCHESTRA.
I.D. MAGAZINE AWARDED io360 THE DESIGN
DISTINCTION AWARD FOR INTERACTIVE MEDIA

AND THEY WERE INCLUDED IN THIS
YEAR'S I.D. TOP 40. IN A BRIEF
TIME TECHNOLOGY CREATES NEW DIMENSIONS
FOR EXPRESSION AND COMMUNICATION,
io360 IS BOTH TECHNOLOGICALLY SAVVY
AND TECHNOLOGY DRIVEN.

DESIGN:
SAGMEISTER INC.
PHOTO: TOM SCHIERLITZ
(PREPRESS)

SEPS, TONE & DUO: PREPRESS COMPANY
PRINTING: C-PRINTS & INSTRUCTIONS,
COLDREDGE NYC.

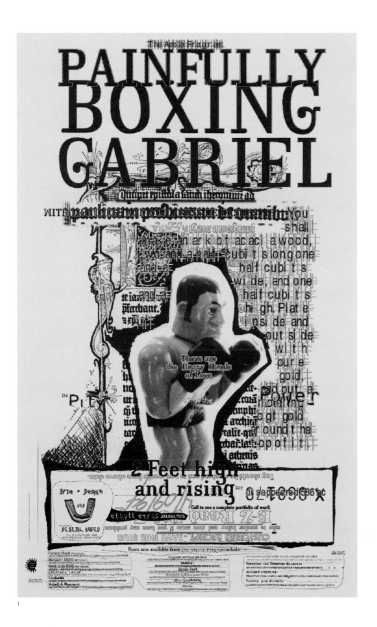

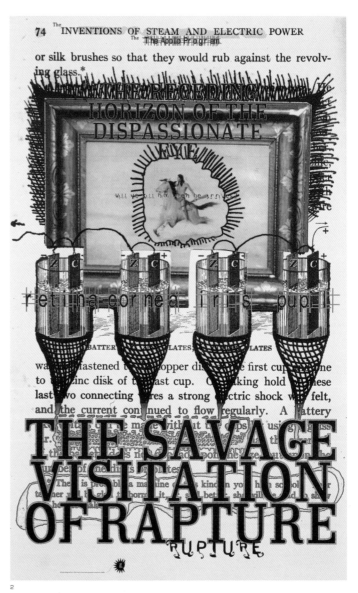

1. *Painfully Boxing Gabriel*

USA 1995 Poster ポスター
CD, P, I: Elliott Peter Earls
CL: The Apollo Program
• Calvino Hand Family, Penal Code

2. *The Savage Visitation of Rapture*

USA 1995 Poster ポスター
CD, P, I: Elliott Peter Earls
CL: The Apollo Program
• Calvino Hand Family, Penal Code

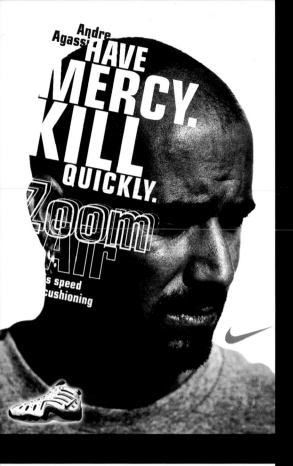

Nike P.O.P. Campaign 1997

The Netherlands 1997 Poster ポスター
CD, AD, D: Jacques Koeweiden
          / Paul Postma
CW: Nike Europe
Digitally Manipulated Images:
Koeweiden Postma Associates
DF: Koeweiden Postma Associates
CL: Nike Europe

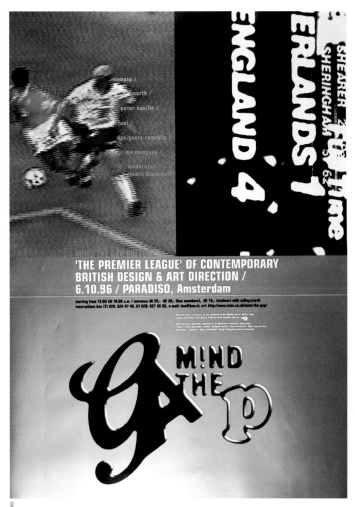

1*

2

1. *"The Iceman Cometh" by Eugene O'Neill*

The Netherlands 1997 Poster ポスター
CD, AD, D: Jacques Koeweiden
　　　　　　/ Paul Postma
P: Los Angeles Police Dept.
CW: Eugene O'Neill
DF: Koeweiden Postma Associates
CL: Theater van het Oosten
• Digitally Manipulated Emigre Font
*→see p217

2. *Mind The Gap*

The Netherlands 1996 Poster ポスター
CD, AD, D: Jacques Koeweiden
　　　　　　/ Paul Postma
CW: Mind The Gap
P, DF: Koeweiden Postma Associates
CL: Mind The Gap
• Eurostile Condensed

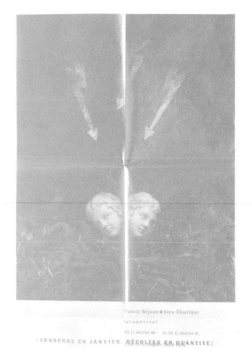

(TONNERRE EN JANVIER, RÉCOLTES EN QUANTITÉ)

Pascal Béjean ● bleu Élastique
(graphiste)
33 1) 403754 90   fx 33 1) 403754 91
E-mail : bleu.elastique@imaginet.fr
Typographie : Denis Majorel

(SI TU TAILLES EN FÉVRIER, TU METTRAS RAISINS AU PANIER)

Pascal Béjean ● bleu Élastique
(graphiste)
33 1) 403754 90   fx 33 1) 403754 91
3 rue de la chapelle 75018 Paris France
E-mail : bleu.elastique@imaginet.fr
Photographie : Denis Majorel
Typographies dessinées par Susan LaPorte

(DE MARS, LA VERDURE EST DE MAUVAIS AUGURE)

Pascal Béjean ● bleu Élastique
(graphiste)

AVRIL

Pascal Béjean ● bleu Élastique
(graphiste)
33 1) 403754 90   fx 33 1) 403754 91
3 rue de la chapelle 75018 Paris France
E-mail : bleu.elastique@imaginet.fr
Photographie : Denis Majorel
Typographies dessinées par Susan LaPorte

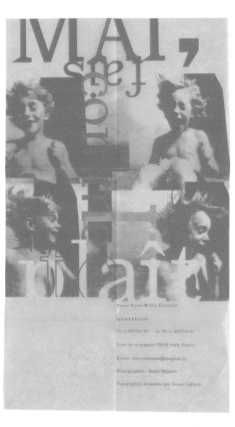

MAI, sers toi, fait

Pascal Béjean ● bleu Élastique
(graphiste)
33 1) 403754 90   fx 33 1) 403754 91
3 rue de la chapelle 75018 Paris France
E-mail : bleu.elastique@imaginet.fr
Photographie : Denis Majorel
Typographies dessinées par Susan LaPorte

Juin des trois habits, n'en garde QU'UN

Pascal Béjean ● bleu Élastique
(graphiste)
33 1) 403754 90   fx 33 1) 403754 91
3 rue de la chapelle 75018 Paris France
http://www.imaginet.fr/~bleuelas/
E-mail : bleu.elastique@imaginet.fr
Photographie : Denis Majorel
Typographies dessinées par Susan LaPorte

Self-Promotional Greeting Cards

France 1996 Poster ポスター
CD, AD, D: Pascal Béjean
P: Denis Majorel
CW: Public Domain
DF, CL: bleu Élastique
Typeface design: Susan LaPorte
● One Iota, Fancy Single, Big Girl,
  Eve Face

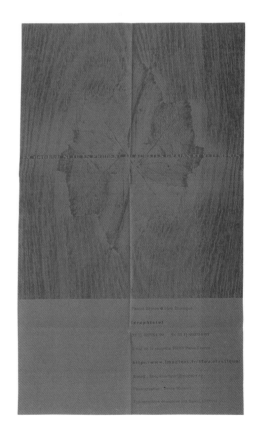

Self-Promotional Greeting Cards

France 1996 Poster ポスター
CD, AD, D: Pascal Béjean
P: Denis Majorel
CW: Public Domain
DF, CL: bleu Élastique
Typeface design: Susan LaPorte
• One Iota, Fancy Single, Big Girl,
  Eve Face

1

2

3

4

Yellow Boots Posters

UK 1997 Poster ポスター
CD, AD, D, I, CW: Rian Hughes
DF: Device
CL: Jun Co.
Typeface design: Device
• Everton, 1.Foonky, 2.Darkside
3.Outlander 4.Vertigo

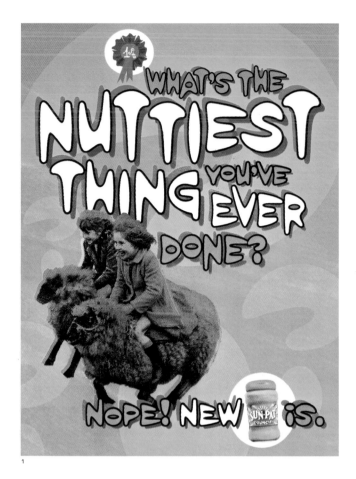

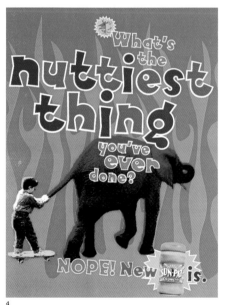

Sun Pat Posters

UK 1996 Poster ポスター
CD, CW: Marcus Vinton
AD, D: Rian Hughes
DF: Device
CL: Sun Pat / Ogilvy + Mathur
Typeface design: Device
• 1.Amorpheus 2.Ainsdale 3.Reasonist
  4.Knobcheese 5.Foonky

1. Hot Dogging and Big Waves

USA 1996 Poster ポスター
AD, D, I, CW: Robynne Raye
DF: Modern Dog
CL: AIGA Hawaii
• Hand lettering

2. 3rd Annual Rainy States Film Festival

USA 1997 Poster ポスター
AD, D, I: Vittorio Costarella
DF: Modern Dog
CL: The Rainy States Film Festival
• Hand lettering

028

1. *Flaming Lips*

USA 1996 Poster ポスター
AD, D, I: Vittorio Costarella
DF: Modern Dog
CL: Moe Cafe
• Fiedler Gothic

2. *Moi, Veuve de L'Empire*

France 1987 Poster ポスター
CD, AD, D: Michel Bouvet
CL: Maison des Arts, Cré'teil

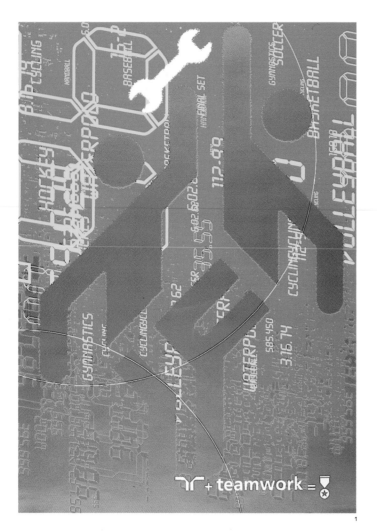

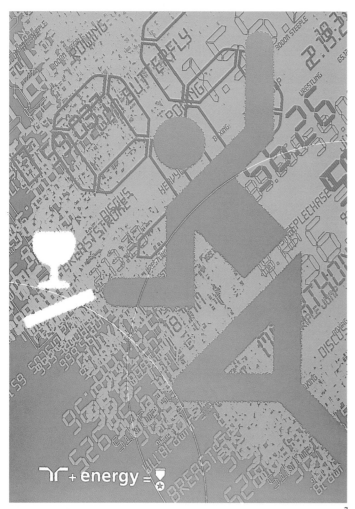

1. *Teamwork*
2. *Speed*
3. *Energy*

The Netherlands 1996 Poster ポスター
CD, AD: Jacques Koeweiden
/ Paul Postma
D: Heike Lunkenheimer
CW: Randstad
DF: Koeweiden Postma Associates
CL: Randstad
• FF Digital

1

2

3

1. *Rapidity*
2. *Flexibility*
3. *Continuity*

The Netherlands 1996   Poster ポスター
CD, AD, D: Jacques Koeweiden
            / Paul Postma
CW: Randstad
P, DF: Koeweiden Postma Associates
CL: Randstad
• 'Copied' Frutiger

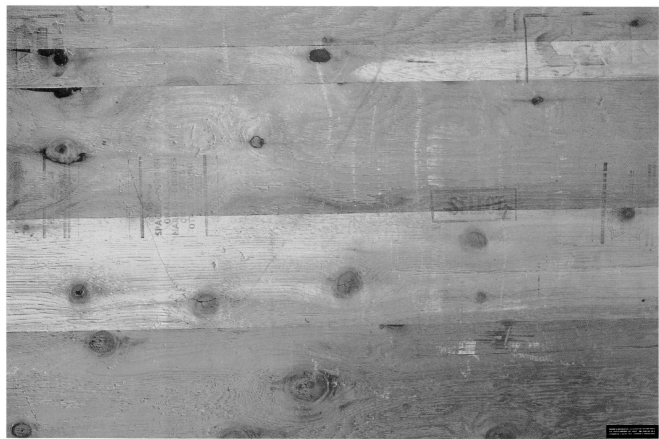

1. **Cahan "Candy-Soda" Poster**

USA 1996 Poster ポスター
CD, AD: Bill Cahan
D, I, CW: Bob Dinetz
P: Holly Stewart
DF: Cahan + Associates
CL: San Francisco Creative Alliance
• Hand lettering

2. **Western Art Directors Club Poster**

USA 1996 Poster ポスター
CD, AD: Bill Cahan
D, I: Bob Dinetz
P: Quantity postcards / David Robin
DF: Cahan + Associates
CL: Western Art Directors Club
• Caslon, Trade Gothic Heavy

3. **Cahan "It's No Secret" Poster**

USA 1996 Poster ポスター
CD, AD: Bill Cahan
D, CW: Craig Clark
DF: Cahan + Associates
CL: San Francisco Creative Alliance
• Futura

4. **Oracle Open World Poster "Advice"**

USA 1996 Poster ポスター
CD, AD: Bill Cahan
D, I, CW: Bob Dinetz
DF: Cahan + Associates
CL: Oracle
• Futura

2

3

4

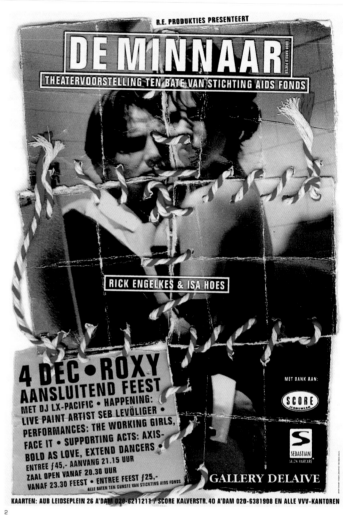

1

2

1. Bauhaus Exhibition Poster

Japan 1994 Poster ポスター
AD, D: Hitoshi Nagasawa
DF: Papier Collé S.A.
CL: Kawasaki City Museum
• Helvetica Neue Heavy

2. De Minnaar / The Lover

The Netherlands 1995 Poster ポスター
CD, AD, D: Petra Janssen
            / Edwin Vollebergh
P: Johan Vigeveno
I, DF: Studio Boot
CL: R. E. P.
• Folio

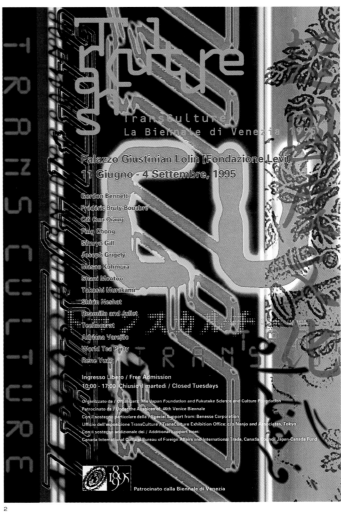

1. *Graphic Arts Message '97*

Japan 1997 Poster ポスター
AD, D: Naomi Enami
I: Giles Rollestone
CL: Too Corporation
• Original font, Franklin Gothic

2. *Trans Culture*

Japan 1995 Poster ポスター
CD: Fumio Nanjo
AD, D: Hiroshi Nakajima
DF: Plank
CL: Venezia Biennale

DR Sign:Age Exhibition Poster

UK 1996 Poster ポスター
CD,AD,D,CW,DF: The Designers Republic
• Dr.Pho-ku, Helvetica 95 Black

1

2

3

1. *Ultramarine*

Switzerland 1996 Poster ポスター
D: Lopetz
DF: Büro Destruct
CL: Reitschule Bern
• ITC Benguiat, Helvetica Neue

2. *Mouse on Mars*

Switzerland 1996 Poster ポスター
D: Lopetz
DF: Büro Destruct
CL: Reitschule Bern
• Büro Destruct -(Cluster)- Font,
  Helvetica Neue Black

3. *Baufest*

Switzerland 1996
Poster ポスター / Flyer フライヤー
D: Lopetz
DF: Büro Destruct
CL: Reitschule Bern
• Helvetica Neue Black, Dot Matrix

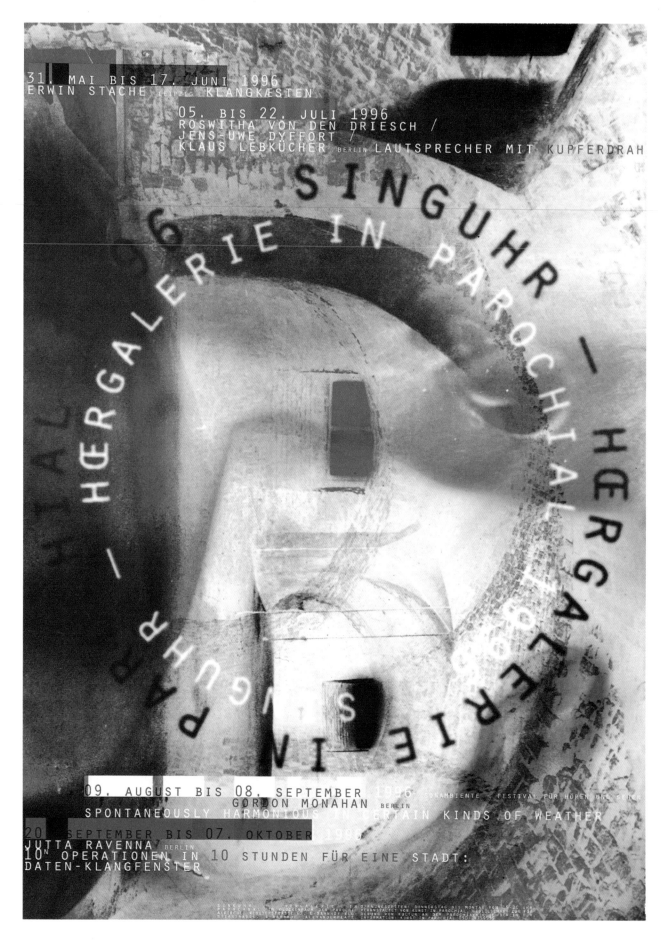

Singuhr, Hœrgalerie in Parochial Kirche

Germany 1996 Poster ポスター
D: Daniela Haufe / Sophie Alex
/ Detlef Fiedler
CW, DF: Cyan
CL: Parochial Kirche Berlin

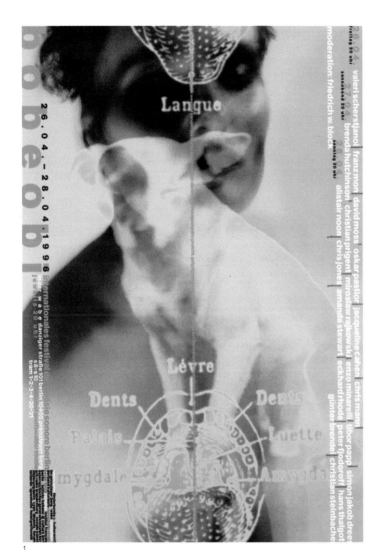

1

2

1. *Bobeobi Nr. 2*

Germany 1996 Poster ポスター
D: Daniela Haufe / Sophie Alex
 / Detlef Fiedler
CW, DF: Cyan
CL: Förderband e.v. Berlin
• Ad Grotesk

2. *Konzert im Bauhaus*

Germany 1994 Poster ポスター
D: Daniela Haufe / Detlef Fiedler
DF: Cyan
CL: Bauhaus Dessau

1

2

3

4

1. Legendary Pink Dots

Switzerland 1996
Poster ポスター / Flyer フライヤー
D: Lopetz
DF: Büro Destruct
CL: Dachstock Reitschule CH-Bern
• BD Medled Regular

2. Exkandalo

Switzerland 1997
Poster ポスター / Flyer フライヤー
D: MBrunner
DF: Büro Destruct
CL: Macroteam
• Zipper

3. MBM Meat Beat Manifesto

Switzerland 1996
Poster ポスター / Flyer フライヤー
D: Lopetz
DF: Büro Destruct
CL: Dachstock Reitschule CH-Bern
• Frutiger, Helvetica

4. 808 State

Switzerland 1996
Poster ポスター / Flyer フライヤー
D: Lopetz
DF: Büro Destruct
CL: Reitschule Bern
• Helvetica Neue

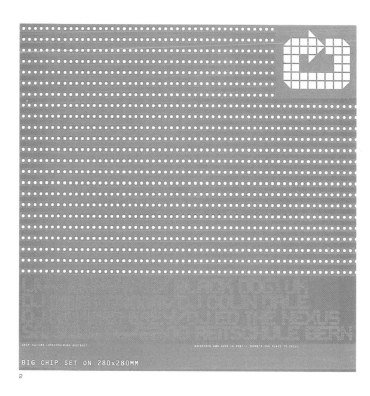

1. Atom Heart

Switzerland 1997
Poster ポスター / Flyer フライヤー
D: Lopetz
DF: Büro Destruct
CL: Reitschule Bern
• Bank Gothic, Bell Gothic

2. Repeat

Switzerland 1996
Poster ポスター / Flyer フライヤー
D: Lopetz
DF: Büro Destruct
CL: Reitschule Bern
• Büro Destruct -〈Brick〉- Font

3. Autechre

Switzerland 1997
Poster ポスター / Flyer フライヤー
D: Lopetz
DF: Büro Destruct
CL: Reitschule Bern
• Buro Destruct -〈LoFi〉- Font, Helvetica Neue

4. Headrillaz

Switzerland 1996
Poster ポスター / Flyer フライヤー
D: Lopetz
DF: Büro Destruct
CL: Wasserwerk Bern
• Amelia, Bell Gothic

Jam Exhibition Poster

UK 1996 Poster ポスター
CD, AD, D: Fabian Monheim
　　　　　／ Sophia Wood
DF: Fly
CL: Barbican Art Gallery
• Compacta

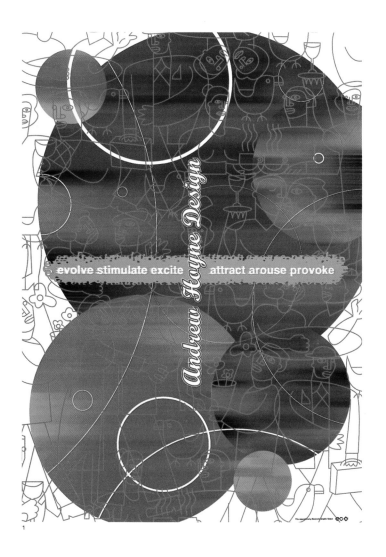

1. **AHD Evolve Poster**

Australia 1997 Poster ポスター
D, CW: Andrew Hoyne
DF, CL: Andrew Hoyne Design
• Script MT, photocopied News Gothic

2. **Bambra Press 6 Colour Poster**

Australia Poster ポスター
CD, AD, CW: Andrew Hoyne
D: Robert Connelly
P: Elli Ianou
DF: Andrew Hoyne Design
CL: Bambra Press
• Bank Gothic, Futura, Gill Sans

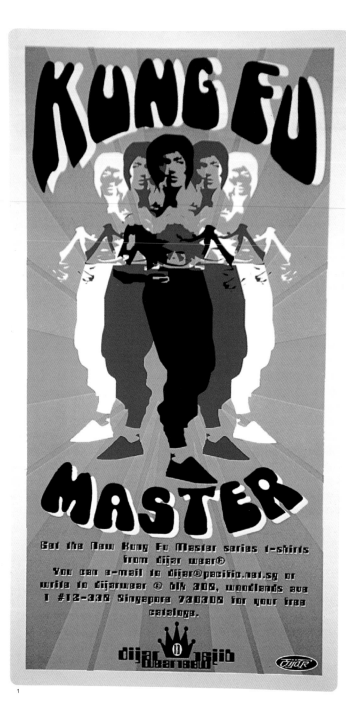

1. **Kung Fu Master**

Singapore 1996 Poster ポスター
D: William Chan
DF: Phunk Studio / Guerilla Fonts
CL: Dijar Clothing
Typeface design: William Chan
(Guerilla Fonts)
• Bollocks

2. **Killa Bash**

Singapore 1996 Poster ポスター
D: Jackson Tan
DF: Phunk Studio / Guerilla Fonts
CL: Independent Rock Concert Organizer
Typeface design: Tzuntat (Guerilla Fonts)
• Killa

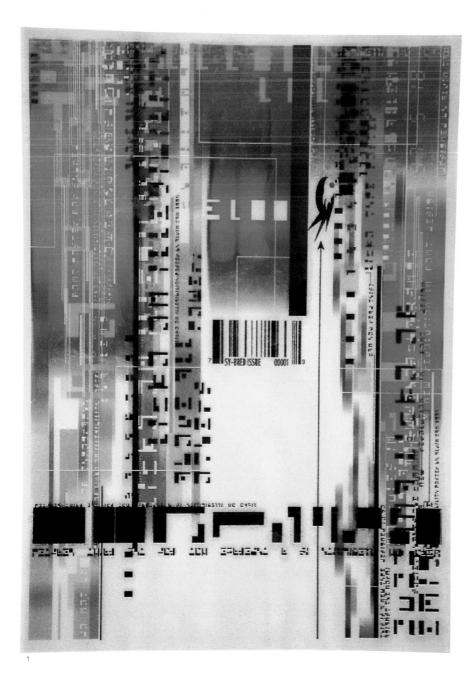

1. *Licko on Illegibility*

Singapore 1996 Poster ポスター
D: Alvin Tan
DF: Phunk Studio / Guerilla Fonts
CL: Guerilla Fonts
Typeface design: Alvin Tan (Guerilla Fonts)
• Licko on Illegibility

2. *Polyester*

Singapore 1997 Poster ポスター
D: Jackson Tan / Alvin Tan
 / William Chan
DF: Phunk Studio / Guerilla Fonts
CL: Guerilla Fonts
Typeface design: Tzuntat (Guerilla Fonts)
• Polyester

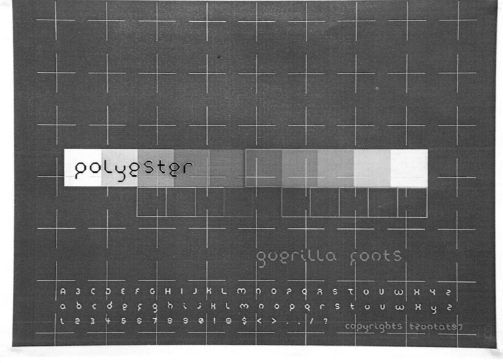

1

2

1

1. *Lucky 13 / Stoltze Lecture Poster*

USA 1997 Poster ポスター
CD, AD, D, P: Clifford Stoltze
D: Wing Ip Ngan
P: Russ Quackenbush
DF: Stoltze Design
CL: AIGA
• Vitrina, Futana, New Baskerville,
  Bell Gothic

2

2. *Vaughan Oliver AIGA Poster*

USA 1995 Poster ポスター
CD, AD, D: Clifford Stoltze
D: Peter Farrell
I: Bina Altera
DF: Stoltze Design
CL: American Institute of Graphic Arts
• Scala, Folio, Poster Bodoni

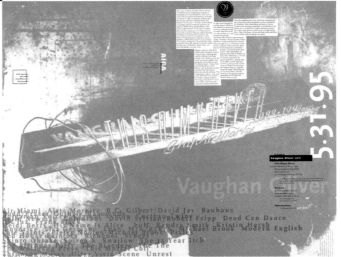

1. *Dance Space*

Singapore 1995 Poster ポスター
CD: Edmund Wee
D: Paul Van Der Veer
DF: Epigram
CL: The Substation
• Truth, Matrix Script

1

2

2. *Fringe Feast!*

USA 1997 Poster ポスター
CD: Michael Olich
AD, D, I: Michael Strassburger
DF: Modern Dog
CL: Seattle Fringe Theatre
• Franklin Gothic, Broadcast

1. *Art Amsterdam 96 (Festival Logo)*
The Netherlands 1996
Poster ポスター / Catalog カタログ
CD, AD: Jacques Koeweiden
        / Paul Postma
D: Anneke Krull
P, DF: Koeweiden Postma Associates
CL: Art Amsterdam
• News Gothic, Bell Gothic

2. *Smelly*
Switzerland 1996 Poster ポスター
D: Lopetz / Heiwid
DF: Büro Destruct
CL: Self promotion
• Gogo Big

1

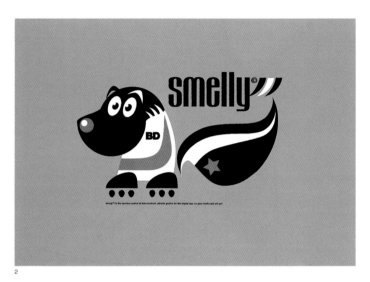

2

1,3. *Promotional Posters*
for Deeper Mixed Tapes

Canada 1997 Poster ポスター
CD, AD, D: Noël Nanton
DF: Typotherapy + Design
CL: DJ Kevin Williams
• Rotis, Bell Gothic

2. *Festa Major UAB 94*

Spain 1994 Poster ポスター
CD, D: Lluis Jubert
AD, D, I: Ramon Enrich
P: Ramon Pallarès
CW, DF: Espai Grafic
CL: Universitat Autonoma de Barcelona
• Dinamoe

1

2

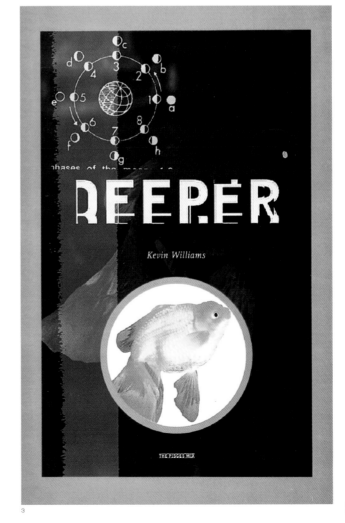

3

Experimental Studio Dessau

Germany 1993 Poster ポスター
D: Daniela Haufe / Detlef Fiedler
DF: Cyan
CL: Bauhaus Dessau

White Elephant

Germany Poster ポスター
D: Daniela Haufe
DF: Cyan
CL: Gallery White Elephant

1. Dog

UK 1995 Poster ポスター
CD, AD, D, P, I, CW: Sean O'Mara
DF: Xon Corp
CL: Self published

2. Festival Joods Iraelische Muziek

The Netherlands 1997 Poster ポスター
CD, AD, D: J.J.F.G. Borrenbergs
　　　　　／ R. Verkaart
CL: Conservatorium

MUSÉE
D'ART
MODERNE
DE LA
VILLE
DE PARIS
20
FÉVRIER-
25
MAI

MUSÉE
DES
MONUMENTS
FRANÇAIS
24
JANVIER-
15
AVRIL

CINÉMA-
THÈQUE
FRANÇAISE
PALAIS
DE CHAILLOT
29
JANVIER-
30
MARS
1997

COLLINE DE CHAILLOT

1

2

1. *The Firties*

France 1997 Poster ポスター
CD, AD, D: Philippe Apeloig
DF: Apeloig Design
CL: Colline de Chaillot
• Futura, Bifur

2. *Exhibition, The Architecture in the Firties*

France 1997 Poster ポスター
CD, AD, D: Philippe Apeloig
DF: Apeloig Design
CL: Musee des Monuments Francais
• Bifur, Futura

3. *A Festival "Octobre"*

France 1997 Poster ポスター
CD, AD, D: Philippe Apeloig
DF: Apeloig Design
CL: Octobre en Normandie
Typeface Design: Philippe Apeloig

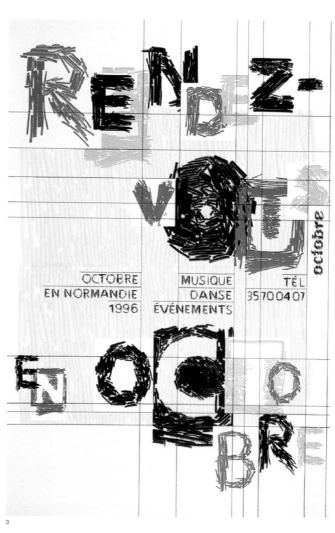

3

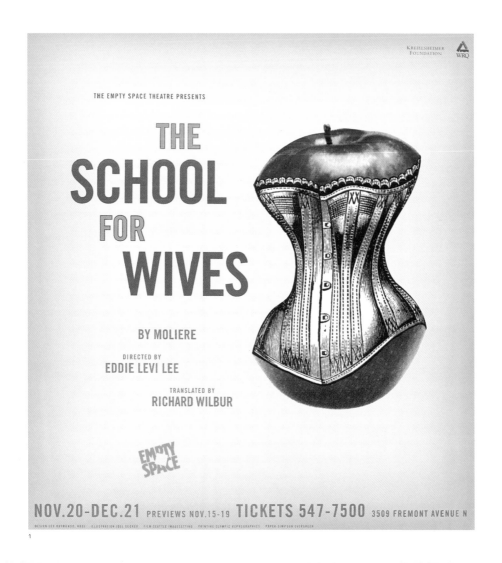

1

2

1. *The School for Wives*

USA 1996 Poster ポスター
D: Leo Raymundo
I: Joel Decker
DF: NBBJ Graphic Design
CL: Empty Space Theatre
• Interstate

2. *Concert de Nadal*

Spain 1997 Poster ポスター
CD, D: Lluis Jubert
AD, D: Ramon Enrich
P: Roger Velázquez
CW, DF: Espai Grafic
CL: Universitat de Barcelona
• Rotis Semi Serif, Franklin Gothic

1

1. *Syracuse University Presents*

USA 1997 Poster ポスター
AD, D, CW: Robynne Raye
DF: Modern Dog
CL: Syracuse University
• Fluorine, Egeltine, Barnum Block,
  Old Wood Block Type

2. *Good Jobs*

Japan 1997 Poster ポスター
AD, D, P: Isamu Nakazawa
I: Kyoko Osada
DF: Hi Hat Studio
CL: Kyoko Osada
• Kyoko Bold, Mambo Bold

2

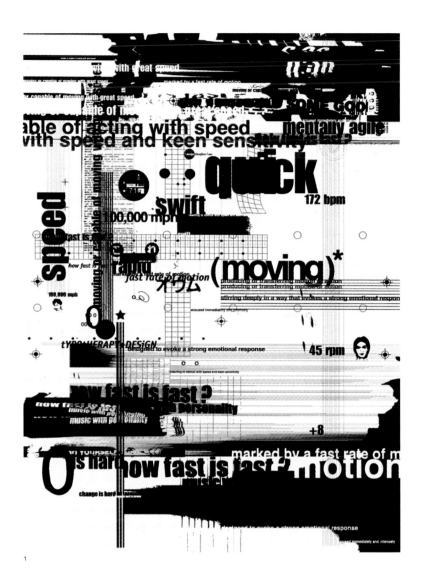

1. *How Fast Is Fast?*

Canada 1997 Poster ポスター
CD, AD, D: Noël Nanton
DF: Typotherapy + Design
CL: 52 Inc.
• Helvetica, Impact, Officina Sans

2. *Radiateur® fontes poster*

France 1995 Poster ポスター
CD, AD, D: Jean-Jacques Tachdjian
DF: i comme image
CL: Radiateur® fontes
• Radiateur® fontes

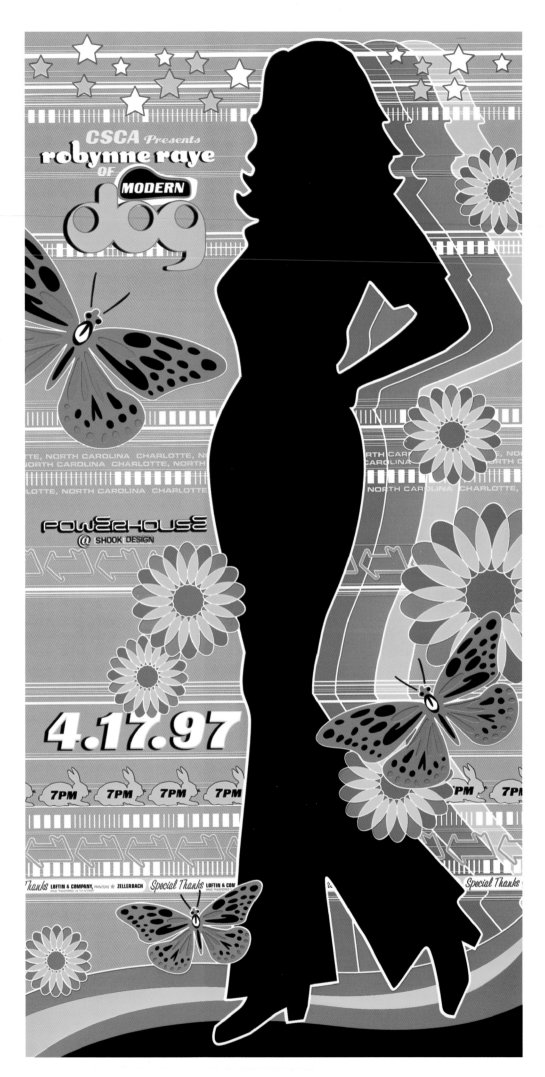

CSCA Presents...

USA 1997 Poster ポスター
AD, D, I: Robynne Raye
DF: Modern Dog
CL: Charlotte Society of Communicating Arts
• Euphoric, Beanstalk, Chatten,
  Inspecteur Clouseau

1. *The Jimi Hendrix Museum Rock Arena*
at Bumber Shoot

USA 1994 Poster ポスター
CD: Susan Pierson
AD, D, I: Michael Strassburger
DF: Modern Dog
CL: Experience Music Project
• Hand lettering

1

2

2. *Model Search '96*

The Netherlands 1996 Poster ポスター
CD, AD, D: Petra Janssen
　　　　　／ Edwin Vollebergh
I, DF: Studio Boot
CL: Creative Connections
• Hand-written, The Free Willie

Cahan "Simple/Complex" Poster

USA 1996 Poster ポスター
CD, AD: Bill Cahan
D, I: Sharrie Brooks
DF: Cahan + Associates
CL: San Francisco Creative Alliance
• New Century Schoolbook

1. *GYMNASTICS*

Switzerland 1997
Poster ポスター / Flyer フライヤー
D: Lopetz
DF: Büro Destruct
CL: Reitschule Bern
• Athletico, Machine

2. *Euroscope Festival*

The Netherlands 1994 Poster ポスター
CD, AD, D: Wout de Vringer
DF: Faydherbe / de Vringer
CL: Cinematheek Haags Filmhuis
• Compacta, Ocr-A, Künstler Script

3. *Ter Visie*

The Netherlands 1995 Poster ポスター
D: Edvard Mlinar
DF: Mlinar Design
CL: Fries Museum
• Kabel, Univers, Adobe Garamond

1. *Granule*

France 1996 Poster ポスター
CD, AD, D: Jean-Jacques Tachdjian
DF: i comme image
CL: Raidiateur® Fontes
• Granule

2. *De Opstand der Dingen*

The Netherlands 1995 Poster ポスター
CD, AD, D: Wout de Vringer
I: West 8
DF: Faydherbe / De Vringer
CL: Centrum Beeldende Kunst Dordrecht
• News Gothic, Compacta

1

2

els Tallers de
TEATRE DE LA PLAÇA CÍVICA

l'Aula de
"LOS FIGURANTES"
DE J. SANCHIS SINISTERRA. DIRECCIÓ NÚRIA FURIÓ
DIMARTS 6 DE MAIG A LES 18 H
DIMECRES 7 DE MAIG A LES 13,15 I A LES 18H

Teatre de la
"VARIACIONS
HAMLET"
CREACIÓ COL.LECTIVA A PARTIR DEL TEXT DE SHAKESPEARE
DRAMATÚRGIA I DIRECCIÓ : RAFEL DURAN
DIMARTS 13 DE MAIG A LES 18H
DIMECRES 14 DE MAIG A LES 13,15 I A LES 18H

UAB

"LA DISPUTA"
DE MARIVAUX. DIRECCIÓ: RICARD GÁZQUEZ
DIMARTS 20 DE MAIG A LES 13,15 H I A LES 18H
DIJOUS 22 DE MAIG A LES 18H

ENTRADA GRATUÏTA AMB INVITACIÓ. AFORAMENT LIMITAT

RECOLLIDA D'INVITACIONS

DE DILLUNS A DIVENDRES DE 12 A 14H I DE 16 A 18H A CULTURA EN VIU
EDIFICI D'ESTUDIANTS DE LA PLAÇA CÍVICA (AL COSTAT DEL TEATRE) TEL. 581 27 56
UNA HORA ABANS DE CADA FUNCIÓ AL MATEIX TEATRE

Vicerectorat d'Estudiants
i de Promoció Cultural

CULTURA EN VIU   TEATRE

1

1. **Aula de Teatre**

Spain Poster ポスター
CD, D: Lluis Jubert
AD, D: Ramon Enrich
P, CW, DF: Espai Grafic
CL: Universitat Autonoma Barcelona
• Scala Sans

2. **Wealthy is the person who reigns**
   over his own time

Germany 1997 Poster ポスター
CD, AD, D: Detlef Behr
CW: Peter Høeg
CL: Plakation
• Letter Gothic

reichtum
ist, wenn du
über deine
eigene zeit
herrschst.

WEALTHY IS THE PERSON WHO REIGNS OVER HIS OWN TIME.

2

1

2

1. *Barrymore's Ghost*

USA 1997 Poster ポスター
CD: Joel Decker
CD, D, P: Amy Lam
P: Brent Whiting
Production: Derek Beecham
DF: NBBJ Graphic Design
CL: Empty Space Theatre
• Franklin, Courier

2. *Mou-Te*

Spain 1996 Poster ポスター
CD, D: Lluis Jubert
AD, D: Ramon Enrich
P: René Jacques
CW, DF: Espai Grafic
CL: Universitat de Girona
• Template Gothic, Scala

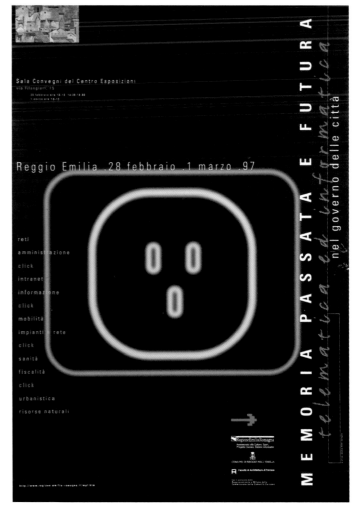

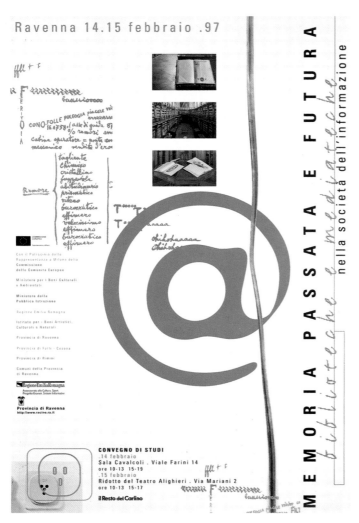

Memoria Passata e Futura - L'Opera
D'Arte Nell'Epoca Digitale e Telematica

Italy 1997　Poster　ポスター
CD, AD, D: Kuni-Graphic Design Company
CL: Regione Emilia-Romagna
• Univers Condensed

Zvi Hecker

Germany 1996 Poster ポスター
D: Andreas Trogisch
DF: Grappa Design
CL: Jüdisches Museum
• Gill

1. Bauhaus Dessau

Germany 1994-96 Poster ポスター
D: Daniela Haufe / Detlef Fiedler
DF: Cyan
CL: Bauhaus Dessau

2. Internationale Kurzfilmtage Oberhausen

Germany 1995 Poster ポスター
D: Heike Grebin / Andreas Trogisch
DF: Grappa Design
CL: Internationale Kurzfilmtage Oberhausen
• Eurostile

3. Internationale Kurzfilmtage Oberhausen

Germany 1994 Poster ポスター
D: Heike Grebin / Tilman Wendland
DF: Grappa Design
CL: Internationale Kurzfilmtage Oberhausen
• Din

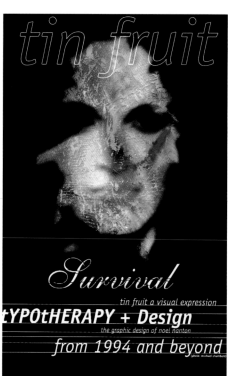

1

1997.3.31 in STORES

KOME KOME CLUB SINGLE COLLETION HARVEST SINGLES 1985-1992

2

1997.6.1 in STORES

『君がいるだけで』を含む全12曲収録

KOME KOME CLUB SINGLE COLLETION HARVEST SINGLES 1992-1997
a K2c ENTERTAINMENT THE LAST SYMPOSIUM   THE BEST SYMPOSIUM
6.21 in STORE   6.21 in STORE

1. *Self Promotion Posters for Art Show*

Canada 1996 Poster ポスター
CD, AD, D: Noël Nanton
P: Michael Chambers
DF: Typotherapy + Design
CL: 52 Inc.
• Officina Sans, Active, Note Book

2. *Kome Kome Club 'Harvest'*

Japan 1997 Poster ポスター
AD, D: Tetsuma Maki
P: Shoji Uchida
CL: Sony Music Entertainment (Japan) Inc.
• Helvetica, Goudy Bold

1

2

3

1. *Impulsen 5*

The Netherlands 1995 Poster ポスター
CD, AD, D: Wout de Vringer
P: Frans van Lent
DF: Faydherbe / De Vringer
CL: Centrum Beeldende Kunst Dordrecht
• Berthold Imago, Compacta

2. *Big Light*

Germany 1995 Poster ポスター
CD, AD, D: Lilly Tomec
P: Olaf Heine
DF: Lilly Tomec Grafik
CL: SPV
• Thesis

3. *Industrial Light & Magic Poster*

USA 1996 Poster ポスター
CD, AD: Bill Cahan
D, I: Michael Verdine
P: Kevin Irby
CW: Teresa Rodriguez
DF: Cahan + Associates
CL: Creative Alliance
• Dinnschriften

1*

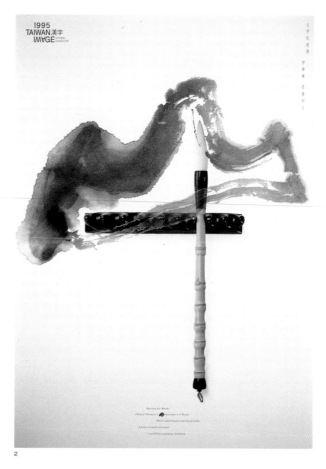

2

3

4

1,2. *1995 Taiwan Image Chinese Character (1. Wind / 2 Mountain)*

Hong Kong 1995 Poster ポスター
CD, D: Kan Tai-keung AD, D: Eddy Yu Chi Kong P: C K Wong Chinese Calligraphy: Yung Ho Yin DF, CL: Kan & Lau Design Consultants
∗→see p217

3,4. *Bornfree Recycled Paper Series Walking Free, Sitting Free, Sleeping Free, Eating Free, Playing Free & Feeling Free*

Hong Kong 1997 Poster ポスター
CD, AD: Kan Tai-keung AD, D: Eddy Yu Chi Kong D: Benson Kwun Tin Yau / Leung Wai Yin P: C K Wong Chinese Calligraphy: Chui Tze Hung / Yung Ho Yin
Computer Illustration: Benson Kwun Tin Yau / John Tam Mo Fai DF: Kan & Lau Design Consultants CL: Tokushu Paper Manufacturing Co., Ltd.

1

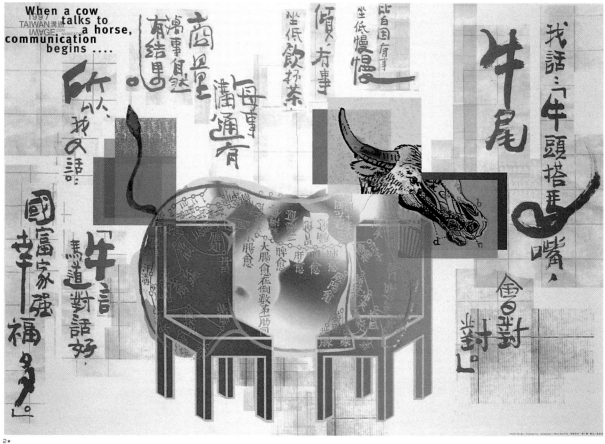

2*

1. *Mountain & Ocean*

Hong Kong 1996 Poster ポスター AD, D: Freeman Lau Siu Hong D: Veronica Cheung Lai Sheung Computer Illustration: Benson Kwun Tin Yau
DF: Kan & Lau Design Consultants CL: Zuni Icosahedron

2. *1997 Taiwan Image Communication-When a Cow Talks to a Horse, Communication Begins...*

Hong Kong 1997 Poster ポスター
AD, D: Freeman Lau Siu Hong D: Fanny Ng Wai Han Calligraphy: Kwok Mang Ho DF, CL: Kan & Lau Design Consultants
*→see p217

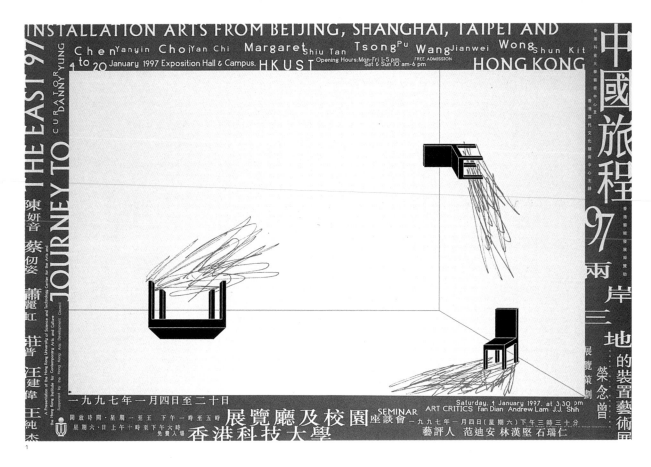

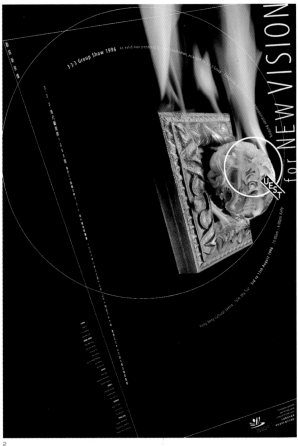

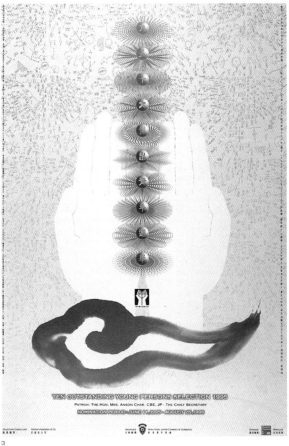

1. *Journey to the East 97 - Installation Arts
from Beijing, Shanghai, Taipei, Hong Kong*

Hong Kong 1997　Poster　ポスター
AD, D: Freeman Lau Siu Hong
D: Joseph Leung Chun Wai
DF: Kan & Lau Design Consultants
CL: Zuni Icosahedron

2. *3.3.3 Group Show 1996*

Hong Kong 1996　Poster　ポスター
AD, D: Freeman Lau Siu Hong
D: Chau So Hing
P: C K Wong
DF: Kan & Lau Design Consultants
CL: 3.3.3 Group

3. *Ten Outstanding Young Persons
Selection 1995*

Hong Kong 1995　Poster　ポスター
CD, AD, I: Kan Tai-keung
D: Fanny Ng Wai Han
DF: Kan & Lau Design Consultants
CL: Hong Kong Junior Chamber of Commerce

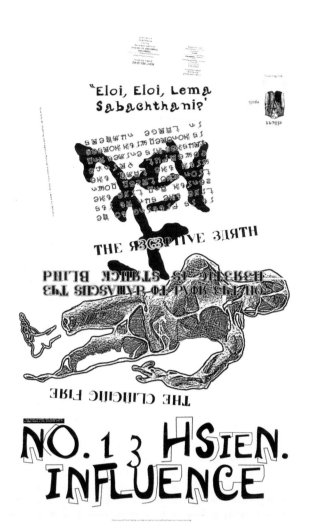

1. *No. 13 Hsien. Influence*

USA 1994 Poster ポスター
CD, P, I: Elliott Peter Earls
CL: The Apollo Program
• Toohey and Wynand, Mothra Paralax

2. *Dysphasia - The Illogical as Gateway to Enlightenment*

USA 1995 Poster ポスター
CD, P, I: Elliott Peter Earls
CL: The Apollo Program
• Dysphasia Family

3. *The Conversion of Saint Paul*

USA 1994 Poster ポスター
CD, P, I: Elliott Peter Earls
CL: The Apollo Program
• Mothra Paralax, Troopship

Seybold Seminars Tokyo 96

Japan 1996 Poster ポスター
AD, D: Tadanori Yokoo
CL: Soft Bank Expo Japan
• Helvetica Bold, Heisei Mincho

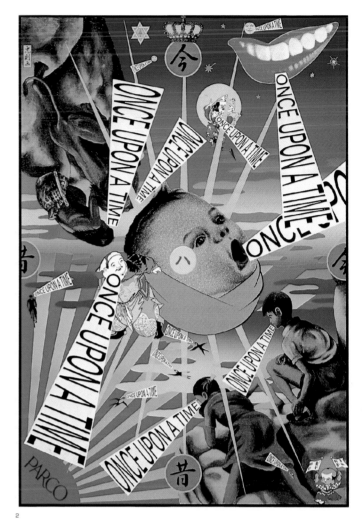

*1. **Katsumi / Devotion***

Japan 1997 Poster ポスター
AD: Tadanori Yokoo
DF: Studio Magic Co., Ltd.
CL: WEA Japan
• Helvetica Bold

*2. **Once Upon a Time***

Japan 1996 Poster ポスター
AD, D, Artwork: Tadanori Yokoo
CL: PARCO Co., Ltd.
• Helvetica, Gyosho CCM

*3. **Miami Modernism***

USA 1995/96/97 Poster ポスター
CD, AD, D, I: John Sayles
DF: Sayles Graphic Design
CL: Caussin Productions
• Hand-rendered

Moschino Poster

USA 1997 Poster ポスター
CD, AD, D: Robert Bergman-Ungar
P: Platon
DF: Bergman-Ungar Associates
CL: Moschino

1. *Perspectives on Los Angeles:*
Narratives, Images, History

USA 1995　Poster ポスター
CD, D: Lisa Nugent
P: Dennis Keeley
DF: ReVerb
CL: The Getty Research Center
• Alternative Gothic, Scala Sans

1

2. *Senior Lottery*

USA 1993　Announcement アナウンスメント
CD, AD, D, P: Ryan J. McGinness
CL: Forbes Gallery

2

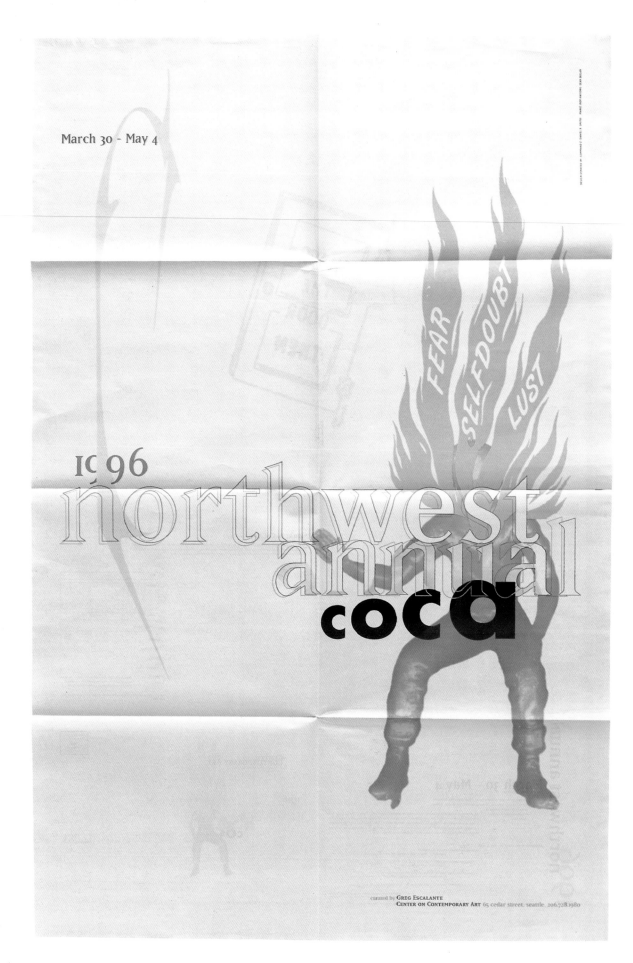

March 30 - May 4

IC 96
northwest annual
coca

FEAR SELFDOUBT LUST

curated by GREG ESCALANTE
CENTER ON CONTEMPORARY ART 65 cedar street. seattle. 206.728.1980

Center on Contemporary Art 1996
Northwest Annual

USA 1996 Poster ポスター ／ Mailer メール
CD, AD, D: Daniel R. Smith
DF: Command Z
CL: Center on Contemporary Art
• Matrix, Futura

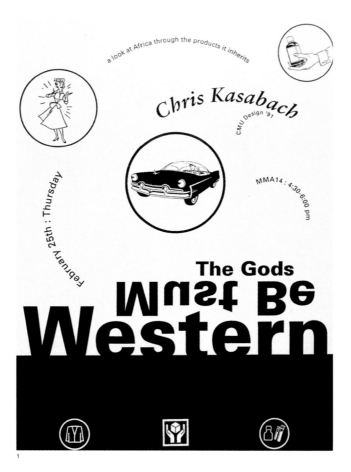

1. **The Gods must be Western**

USA 1993
Announcement アナウンスメント
CD: Dan Boyarski
AD, D, CW, DF: Ryan J. McGinness
CL: Carnegie Mellon University

2. **Concert de Primavera**

Spain Poster ポスター
CD, D: Lluis Jubert
AD, D: Ramon Enrich
P, CW, DF: Espai Grafic
CL: Universitat Autonoma Barcelona
• Matrix Script, Univers 45, Trajan

1

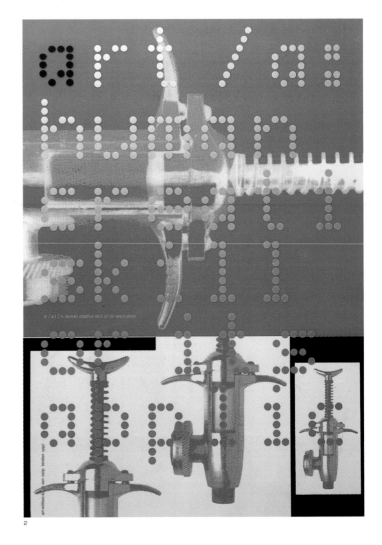

2

3

4

5

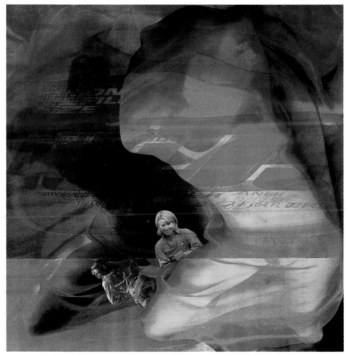

1. *Anne Hung Spring / Summer*
Collection 1997

Canada 1996 Poster ポスター
CD, AD, D: Noel Nanton
P: Ed Chin
DF: Typotherapy + Design
CL: Anne Hung Fashion Designs Inc.
• Helvetica Neue

2. *Art*

UK 1997 Poster ポスター
CD, AD, D, I, CW: Sean O'Mara
P: Matt Shave
DF: Xon Corp
CL: Collen MacMahon
• Dot Matrix

3. *10 Jahre Dampfzentrale*

Switzerland 1997
Magazine advertising 雑誌広告
D: MBrunner
DF: Büro Destruct
CL: Dampfzentrale Bern
• Trade Gothic

4. *Campus de la UDG*

Spain 1997 Poster ポスター
CD, D: Lluis Jubert
AD, D: Ramon Enrich
P: UDG.
CW, DF: Espai Grafic
CL: Universitat de Girona
• Barmeno, Arbitrary

5. *Bleach 409 Society*

USA 1996 Poster ポスター
CD, AD, D, P, I, CW: Jim Poore
DF: Poore House Design
CL: Stacey McElderry
• Helvetica, Franklin Gothic

Blue Cathode Masks

USA 1996
Experimental typeface design
ポスター（タイプフェイスデザイン）
CD. AD. D, P, CW: Liisa Salonen
DF: Cranbrook Academy of Art Design Studio
CL: Liisa Salonen (Self-published)
Typeface Design: CodeBlue by Liisa Salonen
• CodeBlue, Letter Gothic
∗→see p217

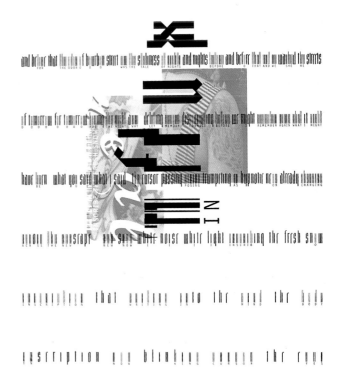

1

2

3

1. Code Blue

USA 1996
Experimental typeface design
ポスター（タイプフェイスデザイン）
CD, AD, D, P, CW: Liisa Salonen
DF: Cranbrook Academy of Art Design Studio
CL: Liisa Salonen (Self-published)
Typeface Design: CodeBlue by Liisa Salonen
• CodeBlue, Letter Gothic

2. In Flux

USA 1996
Experimental typeface design
ポスター（タイプフェイスデザイン）
CD, AD, D, P, CW: Liisa Salonen
DF: Cranbrook Academy of Art Design Studio
CL: Liisa Salonen (Self-published)
Typeface Design: CodeBlue by Liisa Salonen
• CodeBlue, Letter Gothic

3. Hot Dogs

USA 1996
Experimental typeface design
ポスター（タイプフェイスデザイン）
CD, AD, D, P, CW: Liisa Salonen
DF: Cranbrook Academy of Art Design Studio
CL: Liisa Salonen (Self-published)
Typeface Design: CodeBlue by Liisa Salonen
• CodeBlue, Letter Gothic

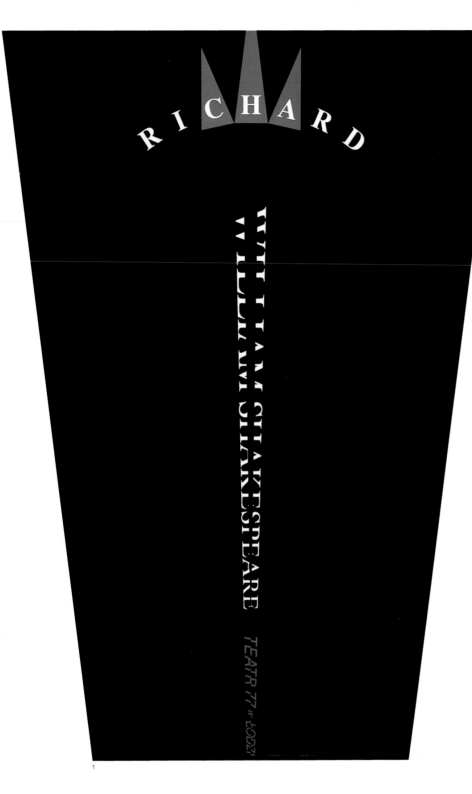

1

1. **Richard III, William Shakespeare**

Poland 1995 Poster ポスター
CD, AD, D, CW: Tadeusz Piechura
DF: Atelier Tadeusz Piechura
CL: Theatr 77

2. **Exhibition of Vitra Design Museum**
Citizen Office, Office of The Future
Ideas and Notices on A New Office World

Poland 1996 Poster ポスター
CD, AD, D: Tadeusz Piechura
CW: Piotr Kloda
DF: Atelier Tadeusz Piechura
CL: Art & Design Society

TEATR WIELKI w ŁODZI, 29 LISTOPADA 1996

Jazz Grand Prix Melomani '95

Poland 1996 Poster ポスター
CD, AD, D: Tadeusz Piechura
CW: Ireneusz Kowalewski
DF: Atelier Tadeusz Piechura
CL: Jazz Society "Melomani"

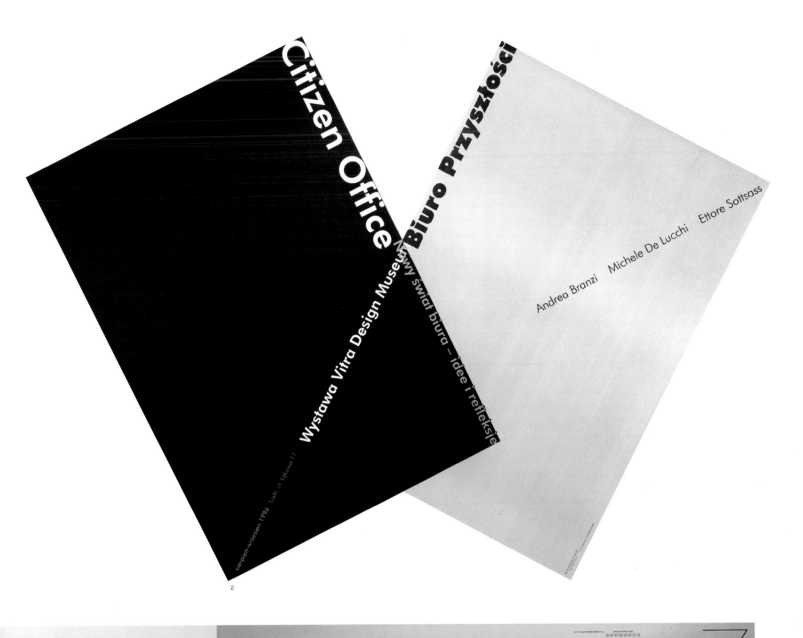

Citizen Office

Biuro Przyszłości

Wystawa Vitra Design Museum

Nowy świat biura – idee i refleksje

Andrea Branzi   Michele De Lucchi   Ettore Sottsass

sierpień-wrzesień 1996   Łódź ul. Łąkowa 11

2

GRAND PRIX MELOMANI '95

TEATR WIELKI w ŁODZI, 29 LISTOPADA 1996

Maywa Denki Tsukuba Expo

Japan 1996 Ticket チケット / Poster ポスター
AD: Norio Nakamura
D: Hiromi Watanabe
P: Jun Mitsuhashi
CL: Sony Music Entertainment (Japan) Inc.

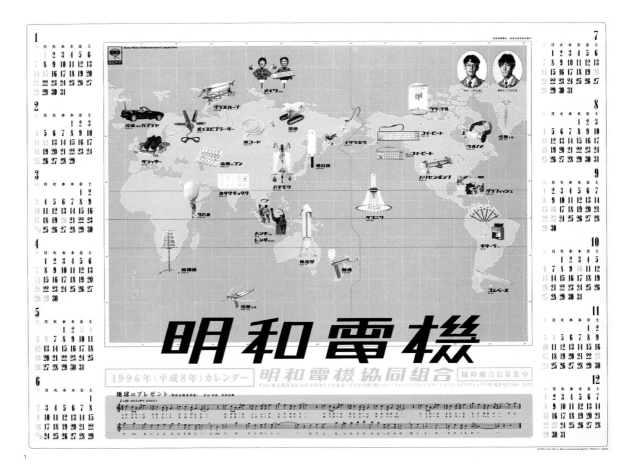

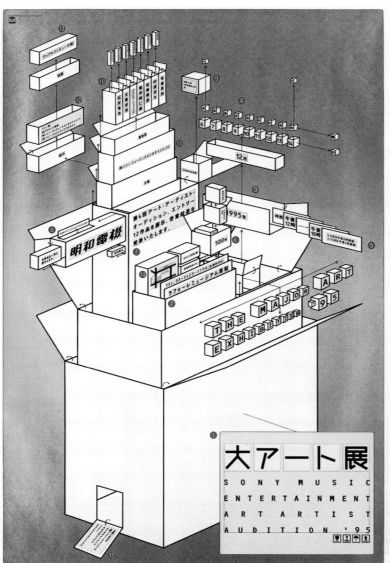

1. *Maywa Denki Calendar*

Japan 1995 Calendar カレンダー
AD: Norio Nakamura
D: Hiromi Watanabe
P: Jun Mitsuhashi
CL: Sony Music Entertainment (Japan) Inc.

2. *The Major Art Exhibition*

Japan 1995 Poster ポスター
AD: Norio Nakamura
D: Hiromi Watanabe
CL: Sony Music Entertainment (Japan) Inc.

DR Interform Calendar 1997

UK 1996 Calendar カレンダー
CD,AD,D,P,I,CW,DF
  : The Designers Republic
Producer: CWC, Tokyo/Interform
• (1) Helvetica Roman
  (2) Dr.Pho-ku
  (3) Handel Gothic, Eurostile,
      Helvetica Roman, Helvetica Bold
  (4) Compacta Bold Italic,
      Helvetica 95, Helvetica
  (5) Ocr-A, Bell Gothic, Orbit-B
  (6) Helvetica Roman
  (7) Eurostile, Helvetica Roman

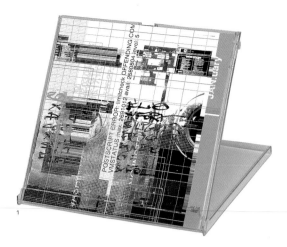

1

2

3

4

5

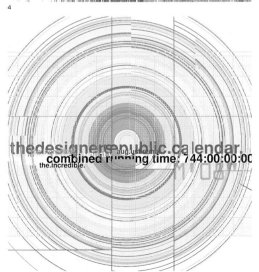

6

7

Calendrier 1997

France 1997 Calendar カレンダー
CD, AD, D, I: Jean-Jacques Tachdjian
P: Jean-Pierre Duplan
DF, CL: i comme image
• Radiateur® fontes

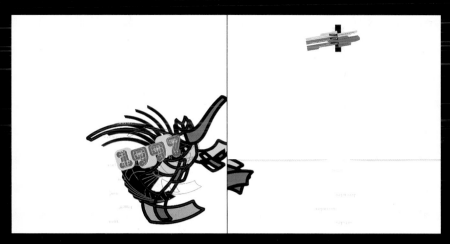

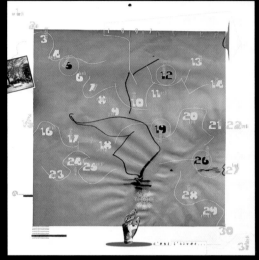

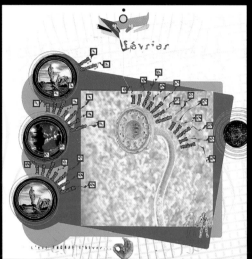

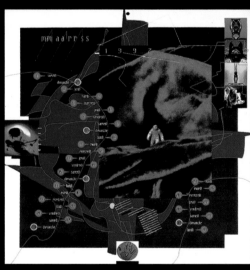

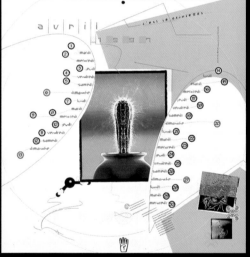

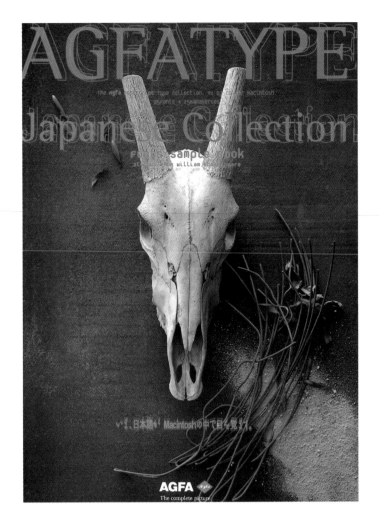

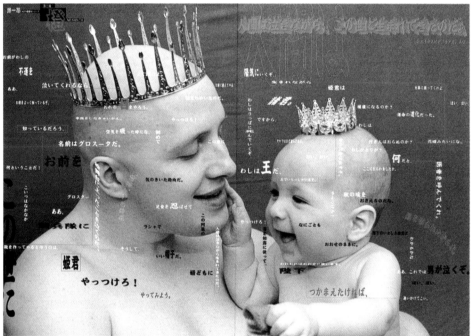

AGFATYPE Japanese Collection Fonts
Sample Book

Japan 1995 Brochure ブローシャ
CD: Yoshi Kubodera
AD, D: Aqui Kuwahara
P: Janos Eifert / Essamba / Shinji Hiraga
/ Karawahn / William King / Tom Maday
/ Yasuhiro Miyahara / David Perry
/ Roy Volkman / Nana Watanabe
CW: Takumi Noda
DF: Connect Inc.
CL: Agfa-Gevaert Japan, Ltd.
• Agfa type

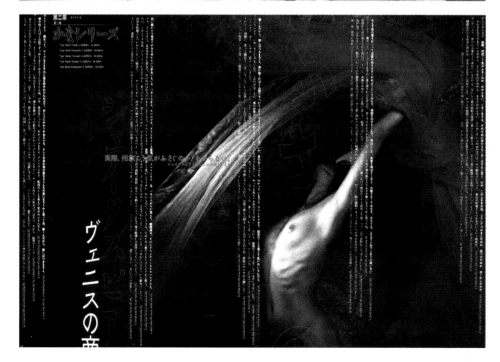

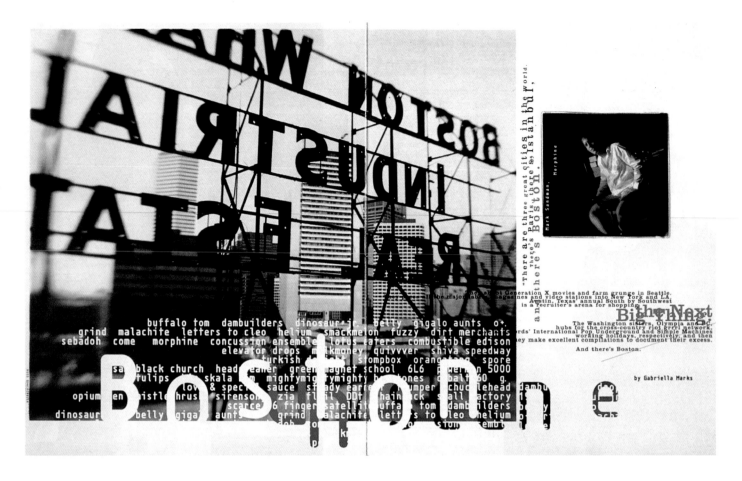

BOSTON WRAL INDUSTRIAL ECTAL

Mark Sandman, Morphine

"There are three great cities in the world, there's Paris, there's Istanbul, another there's Boston."

the major labels, magazines and video stations into New York and LA.
Austin, Texas' annual South by Southwest
is a recruiter's arena for shopping.

BigharNext

The Washington sisters, Olympia and DC, hubs for the cross-country riot grrrl network.
International Pop Underground and Simple Machines working holidays, respectively, and then they make excellent compilations to document their excess.

And there's Boston.

by Gabriella Marks

buffalo tom dambuilders dinosaur jr belty gigalo aunts o.
grind malachite letters to cleo helium smackmelon fuzzy dirt merchants
sebadoh come morphine concussion ensemble lotus eaters combustible edison
elevator drops milkmoney quivvver shiva speedway
turkish stompbox orangutan spore
sa black church head cleaner green magnet school 6L6 piperin 5000
tulips skala ium mightymighty mightymighty bosstones cobalt 60 g.
lov & special sauce steady earnest bumper chucklehead dambu
opium en istle hrusi sirenson zia flail DDt chainlick sall factory 1
scarce 6 finger satellite buffalo tom dambuilders
dinosaur belty gigal aunts grind malachite letters to cleo helium
sebadoh

Boston e

Prescott admits, "I'm absolutely fascinated by Sixties easy listening stuff, and they do it with absolute authority. That's cool because that's an underground that hasn't been tapped. And you know there aren't many places to go to check out stuff and styles that haven't been completely sealed into the ground."

John Dye Of Us
at the Middle East

My dreams are to play New York and have Thurston show up just to see. That to me would be cool

it approaches something dangerously close to bands and women performers

there's an audience for

Boston

Fort Apache

exploring experimental things." Although easily accessible by any transportation or technology, Boston is sufficiently distant from the epicenters of the music business to hear value in and to remain actively receptive to unconventional guests. "In Boston, there's enough of an environment where if you want to pursue something you actually can, and get there with it, try it out, and it doesn't work.

It's a great workshop town. That's why I came back after London and LA. Boston can have a purely creative pur
suit here because it's not an industry town.

There are schools for this but we never quite in keeping with punk."
Paul Kolderie, Fort Apache

from the double decker indie truck tour bybus

Boston Music Scene Feature: Raygun 20

USA 1995 Magazine spread 雑誌 AD: David Carson (Raygun) D: Clifford Stoltze / Peter Farrell
P: Russ Quackenbush Editor: Marvin Scott Jarrett DF: Stoltze Design CL: Ray Gun Magazine
• Isonorm, Claredon

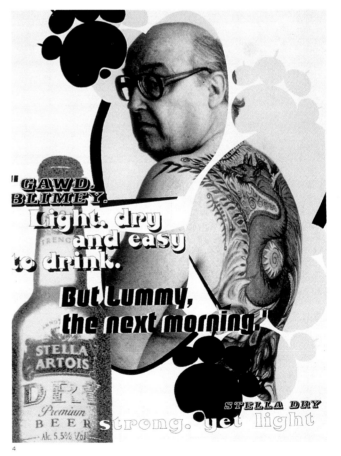

1,2 **Beat**

UK 1995 Magazine 雑誌
CD, AD, D, P, I, CW: Sean O'Mara   DF: Xon Corp   CL: Self-published   • Gill Sans

3,4 **Stella Artois Beer Ads**

USA 1996   Newspaper Advertising 新聞広告
AD: Simon Butler/ Lowe Howard-Spink   D: Somi Kim / Whitney Lowe / Lisa Nugent / James W. Moore   P: Tim O. Sullivan (tattoo)   DF: ReVerb
CL: Lowe Howard-Spink   • Abbess, Altoona, Acropolis, Dolmen, Decorated, Egbert, Enliven, Garage Gothic, Narly, etc.

CAPABILITIES

A solid core of enabling technologies—graphics acceleration, video capture and display, mixed-signal integration, and superior software capabilities—provides for technology leadership.

ESTABLISHING

RELATIONSHIPS

The determination to build relationships with OEMs who determine the features and functionalities they will build into their PCs and with vendors we depend on has been integral to our success.

Trident Microsystems 1995 Annual Report

USA 1995 Annual report アニュアルレポート
CD, AD: Bill Cahan
D: Bob Dinetz
CW: Tim Peters
DF: Cahan + Associates
CL: Trident Microsystems
• Dinnschriften, Univers

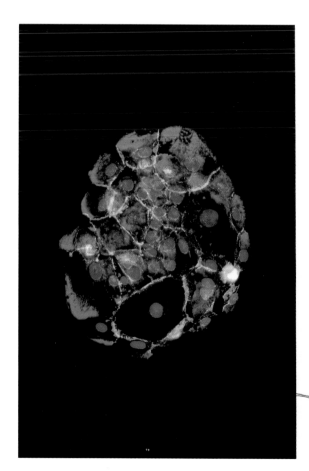

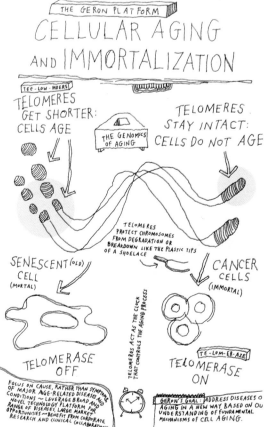

YOU FEEL
THE NEED TO BE
MORE CAREFUL
ABOUT
EVERYTHING.

YOU'RE 74 AND

YOU
BREAK
YOUR
HIP.

MY MOTHER WAS IN A NURSING
HOME FOR FIVE YEARS. IT WAS
NOT GOOD. SHE WOULD LAY
DOWN AND NOT KNOW IF IT WAS
DAY OR NIGHT. I DON'T LIKE
THAT AT ALL.

HELPING THOSE I LOVE
AS I HELP MYSELF.

I CAN KEEP COLORING MY
HAIR, AND IT WILL MEAN
SOMETHING DIFFERENT
THAN WHAT IT MEANS NOW.

I GET MORE
FRIGHTENED
ABOUT
FALLING DOWN.
MAYBE IT'S THE LACK
OF INSURANCE.

BEING
REGARDED
WITH
DISDAIN
BY YOUNGER PEOPLE,
ESPECIALLY IN THIS COUNTRY.

FEAR
OF ILLNESS
AND FEAR OF
DISABILITY.

YOU SPEND LESS MONEY
ON HAIRCUTS.

LESS TIME
TO DO THE
ACTIVITIES
I LIKE TO DO.

WITH AGE COMES SOME NEW
AND DIFFERENT DREAMS,
BUT STILL AS EXCITING AS
IN EARLIER YEARS.

LOSING
YOUR
HEALTH.

Geron 1996 Annual Report - Large Book

USA 1997 Annual report アニュアルレポート
CD, AD: Bill Cahan
D, I: Bob Dinetz
P: Etta Clark / William Mercer McLeod
 / Geron Corp.
I: Lorraine Maschler
CW: Carole Melis
DF: Cahan + Associates
CL: Geron Corporation
• Rosewood Fill, Trade Gothic

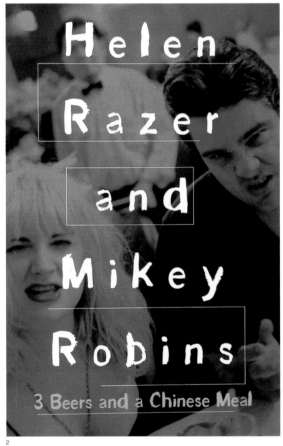

1. *Bongwater*

Australia 1996 Publication 書籍
AD, D: Andrew Hoyne
P: Dean Phipps
DF: Andrew Hoyne Design
CL: Random House
• Mr. Bong

2. *3 Beers & A Chinese Meal*

Australia 1996 Publication 書籍
AD, D: Andrew Hoyne
P: Rob Blackburn
DF: Andrew Hoyne Design
CL: Random House
• Mr. Cleaver

3. *Les Repésentations de Santé des Jeunes*

Belgium 1996 Brochure ブローシャ
AD, D: Francisca Mendonça
I: Nathalie Pollet
DF: Signé Lazer
CL: Belgian Red Cross
• Din-Matrix Script

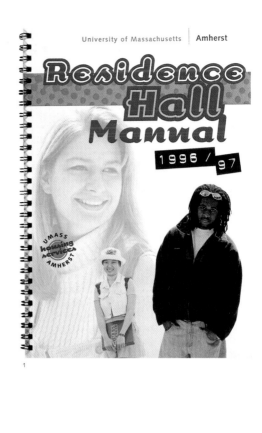

University of Massachusetts | Amherst

Residence Hall Manual
1996 / 97

UMASS
housing services
AMHERST

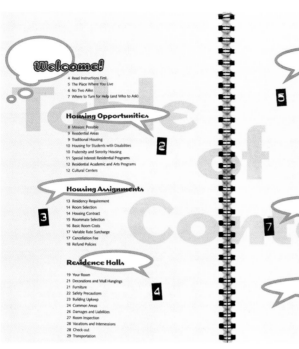

Table of Contents

---

the Year *in* Review

Joey Scouts

Joey Scouting in Victoria is the newest youth section, for girls and boys aged six and seven, and has been going for nearly six years. The rapid increase and continuing community demand for Joey Scouting has led to the creation of many more Joey Mobs.

The highlight of the Joey Scout year was the third Joey Zoo Day held at the Royal Melbourne Zoo, attracting more than 3600 Joey Scouts and their families from all over Victoria. The enormous Joey Scout hop was once not to be forgotten by its young participants; overall the day was a great success and enjoyed by all.

Joey Scouts care for the environment

The new Emironic Joey Scout project encourages young children to plant a native tree, become involved in recycling, learn about our native animals and birds or clean up a park. The project is achieved by working alone, with a Joey Scout Mob or with their families. An Emironic badge is awarded at the end of the project.

Cub Scouts

This year, 1996, is the 80th anniversary of the beginning of Cub Scouting. Cub Scouts are boys and girls aged 8, 9, and 10, and they will wear a special badge to mark the event. The badge is achieved by completing any three fun tasks such as: learning a jungle dance, performing a jungle rap, painting a large jungle mural or making a jungle mask or jungle puppet.

In January more than 1200 Cub Scouts and Leaders attended the ACT Cuboree, the theme was 'Shaping the Future'. Victoria sent 195 members (organised by Hoadley Region) to Camp Cottermouth. Canberra to enjoy this spectacular and creative Cubbing event. All of the activities were aimed at the future, along with lots of fun, dancing, space travel and of course water slides. A Victorian Cuboree will be held in April 1997.

Cub Scouts 'camping under canvas' has been implemented following the Cub Scout Review which recommended that Cub Scouts be permitted to camp under canvas (tents). Such camps provide exciting and challenging activities for Cub Scouts, and the opportunity to learn new skills and really enjoy the fun and excitement of Cubbing in the outdoors.

Scouts

Scouts (aged 11 to 14 years) throughout the world including Scouts from Victoria invaded Holland for the 18th World Scout Jamboree, where more than 25,000 Scouts from 120 countries converged on Dronten, Holland for 10 days of fantastic activities and experiences.

The three major themes of the World Jamboree were: the environment, the future is now and international cooperation. Jamborees are designed to foster international goodwill, friendship and cooperation - with dance, song, food, activities and entertainment. Being part of a World Jamboree is definitely the opportunity of a lifetime for any member of Scouting. The next Australian Jamboree will be held at Springfield, Queensland in January 1998.

Back at home there have been many and varied Scout activities during the year including the Cohen Shield and Stradbroke Cup (competition camping), Scout Ski at Mt Baw Baw, hiking competitions, bike hiking activities, youth forums, camping and many sailing events.

Venturers

Fifty years ago, the Scout Association introduced senior Scouts, known today as Venturers, young people aged 14 to 17 years. Their official anniversary date was 24 February 1996, with many Venturer Units commemorating this milestone with special events and a special 50th anniversary badge.

Venturespect 1995

Approximately 400 Leaders and Venturers took part in a weekend conference and workshops to discuss the National Venturer Section Review. A major highlight was the activities expo with displays of the many and varied Venturer activities.

The Venturer's highest honour, the Queen's Scout Award, was presented by the Governor of Victoria, the Hon. Richard McGarvie to 180 young men and women. To earn the award, hundreds of hours are spent doing community service and personal development, learning skills such as teamwork, leadership, personal confidence, self reliance and of course making friends.

Rovers

Rovers, the senior training section of Scouting, aged between 18 and 26, have now planted more than 2000 trees at their own Malsking Park campsite near Yea. Indigenous trees were planted to provide shelter for campers, and homes for animals and birds. Snowgum stores donated 500 trees towards the environmental project at Malsking.

Popular Rover activities included the Mudbash buggy race (won by Fort Nepean), the annual Rover Ball, Surfmoot held at Anglesea, and skiing at Mt Baw Baw and Bogong High Plains.

The Rover's highest honour, the Baden Powell Award, was presented at Government House by the Governor and Chief Scout of Victoria, the Hon. Richard McGarvie to 14 recipients in October 1995.

The Scout Association of Australia

Victorian Branch
annual report
1995-96

---

1. **UMASS Residence Hall Manual**

USA 1997 Manual マニュアル
AD: Pamela Geddis / Clifford Stoltze
D: Nicole Curran / Wing Ip Ngan
P: Sam Ogden
CW: Martha Maguire
DF: Stoltze Design
CL: University of Massachusetts
• Dogma, Dynamoe

2. **Scouts Annual Report**

Australia 1995
Annual report アニュアルレポート
AD: Andrew Hoyne
D: Rachel Miles / Angela Ho
DF: Andrew Hoyne Design
CL: Scouts Association
• Mr. Scout

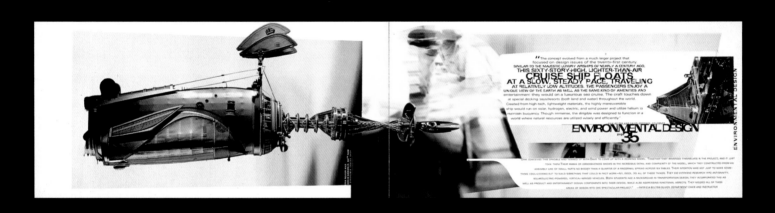

Art Center College of Design Catalog 1997-98

USA 1996 Catalog カタログ
CD: Stuart I. Frolick   AD, D: Darin Beaman   Assoc. Designers: John Choe / Carla Figueroa
P: Steven A. Heller   Production Manager: Ellie Eisner   Editorial Staff: Karen Jacobson / Dana Huebler / Dolores Banerd
DF: Art Center College of Design - Design Office   CL: Art Center College of Design
• Tweeker, Rose Queen, Univer, Letter Gothic

Liberal Arts and Sciences
STEPHEN POTTER, CHAIRMAN.
LIBERAL ARTS AND SCIENCES DEPARTMENT

"More than ever designers must be aware of the social matrix from which they have emerged and in which they will function and CARRY ON THE TRADITION of creativity we call design. New tools and technologies will never replace the imaginative processes which created them. Along with them we carry on the daunting tasks of *humanizing ourselves*, caring for one another in a world of diminishing resources, and caring for the environment—our endangered home. It is the role and responsibility of the Liberal Arts and Sciences Department not only to inform but to stimulate, provoke, and challenge; to remind our students that we co-exist in an endlessly unfolding universe of interconnected metaphors."

LIBERAL ARTS AND SCIENCES PROGRAM

In addition to technical proficiency, a broad understanding and awareness of social, cultural, and scientific issues are vital to the designer. The ethical and environmental implications of a designer's work must also be considered as a major part of this specialized process. The purpose of the Liberal Arts and Sciences program at Art Center (Europe) is to complement the design education with a variety of courses specifically focused to help students meet the increasing demands of the professional world. The program, which draws its faculty and visiting lecturers from the international community, aims to address practical needs while stimulating self-exploration and intellectual curiosity.

For the bachelor of fine arts or the bachelor of science degrees, students must satisfactorily complete 45 units of Liberal Arts and Sciences coursework. Certain courses are required for each major, but the remainder of the units can be selected from a range of offerings in the humanities, social sciences, and natural sciences. Students with a Swiss Maturité, French Baccalauréat, German Arbitur, or their equivalent can transfer some units toward their academic requirements. Units can also be transferred from accredited colleges.

ADS Awareness Seminar, February 1995.

24

COMMUNICATION DESIGN
TOM BLUHM, CHAIRMAN. COMMUNICATION DESIGN DEPARTMENT

"Innovative, intelligent problem solving is at the heart of effective communication design. At Art Center (Europe), Communication Design majors work from the premise that good IDEAS AND SOUND solutions come from life experience, academic knowledge, and a thorough understanding of the marketplaces they will enter as professionals.

An intensive, rigorous curriculum enables students to develop a firm theoretical and practical grasp of the communication process while building a strong foundation of *skills that employ* both traditional methods and electronic technologies. As socially responsible designers, they are well equipped to meet the communication challenges of our rapidly changing world."

Florian Dengler. (D) sixth term. Interactive entertainment magazine of cultural offerings

32

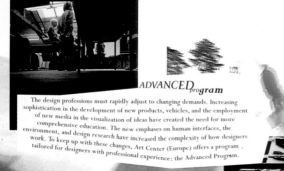

ADVANCED *program*

The design professions must rapidly adjust to changing demands. Increasing sophistication in the development of new products, vehicles, and the employment of new media in the visualization of ideas have created the need for more comprehensive education. The new emphases on human interfaces, the environment, and design research have increased the complexity of how designers work. To keep up with these changes, Art Center (Europe) offers a program tailored for designers with professional experience: the Advanced Program.

ADVANCED PROGRAM

Professional designers and design graduates who seek to enhance their creative skills and design expertise can attend one of Art Center (Europe)'s Advanced Programs. Students pursue an intensive program of studio courses in their chosen major, usually by covering the final three terms (one calendar year) of the regular curriculum. In certain cases, Advanced Program students may take a selection of courses from different term levels sharing their first term to strengthen particular skills before they enter the final two terms. Participants in the Advanced Program often work on sponsored design research projects, which offer them the opportunity to work closely with industry professionals.

Students can also pursue an individualized Advanced Program of only one or two terms. A certificate of completion is awarded at the conclusion of the program. For application information, please see page 58.

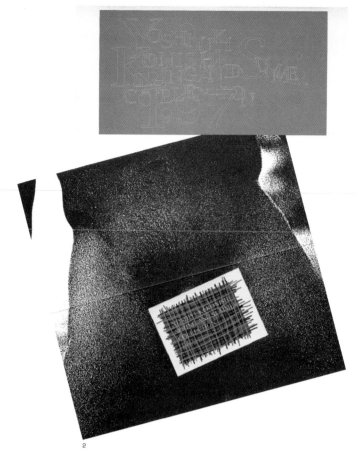

1. *Yoshiyuki Konishi S & S Collection 1997*

Japan 1997 Brochure ブローシャ
CD: Jin Hidaka
CD, AD, D: Takayoshi Tsuchiya
P: Hikaru Kobayashi
CL: Ficce Uomo Co., Ltd.
• New York (modified)

2. *Yoshiyuki Konishi S & S Collection 1997*

Japan 1996 DM ダイレクトメール
CD: Jin Hidaka
CD, AD, D: Takayoshi Tsuchiya
P: Hikaru Kobayashi
CL: Ficce Uomo Co., Ltd.
• New York (modified)

3. *Yoshiyuki Konishi '94 -'95 A & W
   Collection*

Japan 1994 Brochure ブローシャ
CD: Jin Hidaka
CD, AD, D, I: Takayoshi Tsuchiya
P: Takayuki Watanabe
DF: Hidaka Republic
CL: Ficce Uomo Co., Ltd.

"No one in his right mind ignores the New York Shows. It's not just what's on the runway that influences us all. It's the audience, the models, the makeup, the music, the backstage chaos, the frenzy. Sure, you want to check yourself into a padded room at Bellevue by Friday at 6:00. But what wonderful insanity."

—Linda Wells, *Allure*

PHOTO BY RAYMOND MEIER

welcome to the runways.

three photographers capture the collections.

New York Fall Collection '97

USA 1997
Publication 書籍
CD, AD, D: Robert Bergman-Ungar
DF: Bergman-Ungar Associates
CL: CFDA

Word Magazine Issue: May '96

Canada 1996 Magazine spreads 雑誌
CD, AD, D: Noël Nanton
P: Patric Nichols
DF: Typotherapy + Design
CL: Word Magazine
• Self-made, Notebook, Tek 9,
  Gererator 4, F2 State

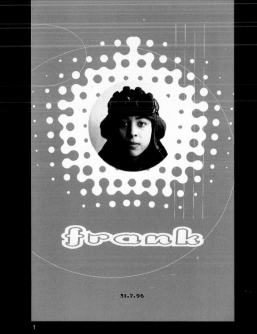

1. **Frank**

UK 1996 Poster ポスター
CD, AD, D, P, I, CW: Seán O'Mara
DF: Xon Corp
CL: Frank
• Dogma

2. **Jobs for the Boys / Jobs for the Girls**

UK 1996 Flyer フライヤー
CD, AD, D, P, I, CW: Seán O'Mara
DF: Xon Corp
CL: Frank
• Dot Matrix

3. **The Internet**

UK 1995 Magazine spread 雑誌
CD, AD, D, P, I, CW: Sean O'Mara
DF: Xon Corp
CL: Creative Review
• Chicago, Ocra

frank

31.7.96

1

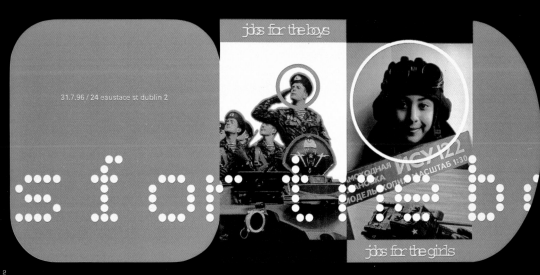

jobs for the boys

31.7.96 / 24 eaustace st dublin 2

jobs for the girls

2

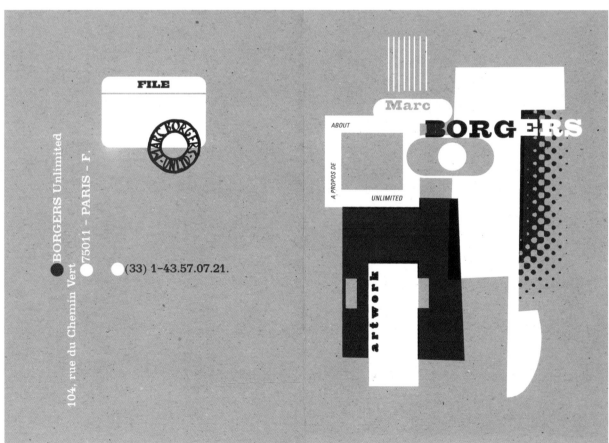

A Propos / About Marc Borgers

France 1996
Cover for promotional folder
プロモーションフォルダー
CD, AD, D, I: Marc Borgers
DF, CL: Borgers Unltd.
Typeface design: Marc Borgers

Werkstatt
Wrksttt
Wksttt
Wsttt
Wkst

radio

Nach einer Vorlage wird eine Platine mit elektronischen Teilen bestückt, gelötet und danach aus PapierMaché ein nach eigenen Vorstellungen gestaltetes Gehäuse drum herum gebaut.

Mit dem Radio können 6 bis 7 Sender empfangen werden.

zeit Donnerstag, 19–22 Uhr
daten 7. mai, 24 Oktober bis 12 Dezember 96
kosten Fr 200.–
material Fr 55.–
leitung Rosmarie Boschetti, Elektrikerin

videobearbeitung für anfängerInnen

Einführung - Material- und Gerätekunde - Codierung des Originalbandes - Kopie des Originalbandes mit sichtbarem Timecode - visionieren und komponieren des Videofilms, dh Schnittliste schreiben - programmieren des Schnittes und Schnitt auf Masterband - Titel schreiben mit Titelgerät - wenn nötig Kommentar sprechen - Musikeinspielungen - Kopieren des Masterbandes auf VHS oder SVHS.

Selbstgedrehten Videofilm auf Kameraskassette mitbringen, System Sony Hi8.

zeit 9-17 Uhr, 1 Stunde Mittagspause
daten 2 Samstage, 26 Oktober und 2 November 96
kosten Fr 120.–, exklusive Material
leitung Heinz Lüscher

Jonglier-Keulen

Delphin short Fr. 26.–

Luna Fr. 33.–

Rainbow Fr. 36.50

Glitzer Fr. 36.50

Circus Training Fr. 38.–

Pirouette

Pirouette Training Fr. 48.–

Pirouette Circus Fr. 56.–

Pirouette Europ Fr. 59.–

Messer Fr. 36.–

Jonglier-Ringe

Ring Fr. 5.50

Ring Moon Fr. 8.50

Kinder-Ring Fr. 4.50

Kinder-Ring Moon Fr. 6.–

Glimmer-Ring Fr. 8.50

UV-Ring Fr. 8.–

Jongliertuch gross Fr. 3.90

Jongliertücher klein Fr. 10.80

Jonglierartikel / Einrad / Drachen // Winterthur / Metzggasse 8

---

1. **Werkstattprogramm**

Switzerland 1996 Brochure ブローシャ
D: Thomas Bruggisser
DF: Grafiktraktor
CL: Daniela Winkler

2. **Jugglux**

Switzerland 1996 Brochure ブローシャ
D: Thomas Bruggisser
DF: Grafiktraktor
CL: Dominique Druey
• Syntax

1. *PUI Magazine*

UK 1996 Magazine 雑誌
CD, AD, D, P, I, CW: Sean O'Mara
DF: Xon Corp
CL: PUI

2. *Evil Dee*

UK 1997 Magazine 雑誌
CD, AD, D, P, I, CW: Sean O'Mara
DF: Xon Corp
CL: Down Low
• Dot Matrix

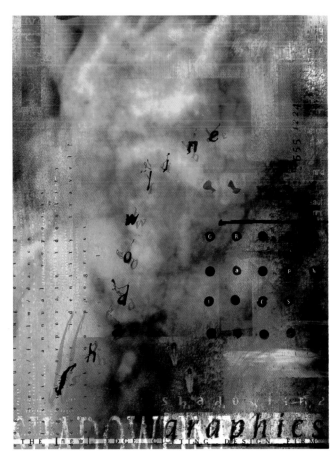

1. **Shadowline Graphics
- The New Edge Cutting Design Firm**

Australia 1996
Magazine advertising 雑誌広告
CD: Royden Irvine
D: Matthew Hatton
DF, CL: Shadowline Graphics
• Stone Informal Semi-Bold,
  Tema Cantante Regular

2. **A Festival "Octobre"**

France 1997 Brochure ブローシャ
CD, AD, D: Philippe Apeloig
D: Daniel Utz
DF: Apeloig Design
CL: Octobre en Normandie
• News Gothics

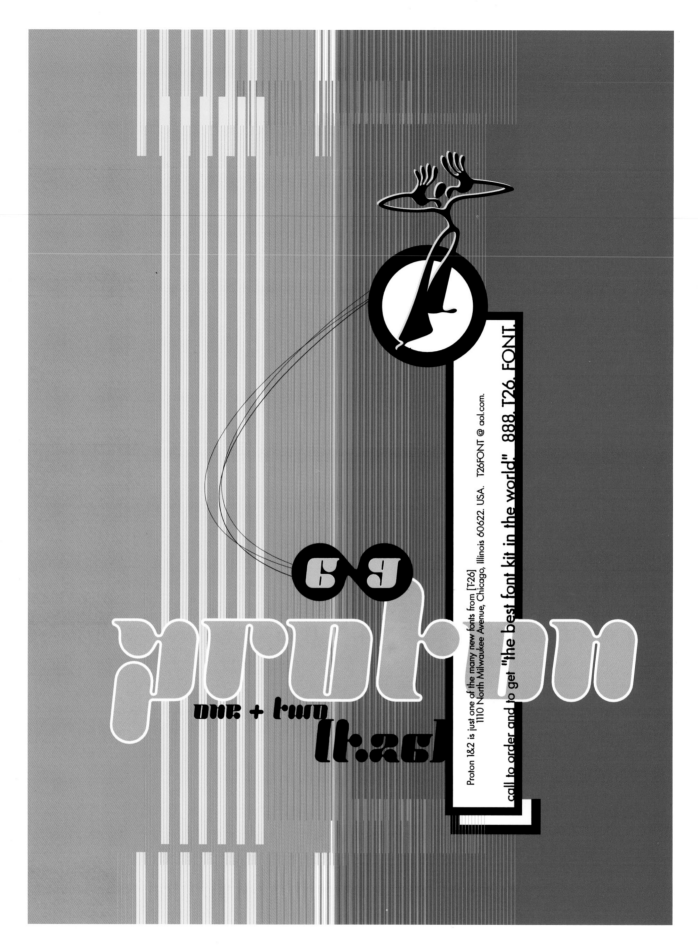

Proton

USA 1997　Magazine advertising　雑誌広告
CD, AD, D, I: Carlos Segura
DF: Segura Inc.
CL: [T-26]
• Proton, Graham

1. **Guerilla Fonts Action Font Kit**

Singapore 1996
Brochure (Self promotion) ブローシャ
D: Jackson Tan / Alvin Tan / William Chan
DF: Phunk Studio
DF, CL, Typeface design: Guerilla Fonts
• Hijack, Bollocks, etc. (Garage Fonts)

2. **In Fonts We Trust**

Singapore 1997
Magazine advertising (Self promotion) 雑誌広告
D: Jackson Tan / Alvin Tan / William Chan
DF: Phunk Studio
DF, CL: Guerilla Fonts
Typeface design: Tzuntat (Guerilla Fonts)
• Hijack (Garage Fonts)

3. **The Alternative Pick**

USA 1996 Campaign キャンペーン
CD, AD, D, I: Carlos Segura
I: Hatch
DF: Segura Inc.
CL: The Alternative Pick
• Boxspring, Mattress

1

2

3

4

1. **Wools of New Zealand Entry**

Australia 1997 Pamphlet パンフレット
AD, D: Andrew Hoyne
D: Rachel Miles
DF: Andrew Hoyne Design
CL: Wools of New Zealand

2. **Symposium Invitation**

Germany 1994 Brochure ブローシャ
CD, AD, D: Detlef Behr
CL: Hoechst AG
• Garamond, Futura

3. **Kolloquium über Bernd & Hilla Becher**

Japan 1996 Publication 書籍
AD: Hitoshi Nagasawa
D: Naoko Yagi
DF: Papier Collé S.A.
CL: Kawasaki City Museum
• Helvetica Neue Heavy

4. **National Computer Board Annual Report 1994-95**

Singapore 1995
Annual report アニュアルレポート
CD: Edmund Wee
D: Paul Van Der Veer
P : Daniel Zheng / Russel Wong
DF: Epigram
CL: National Computer Board (NCB)
• Ocrb, Swift

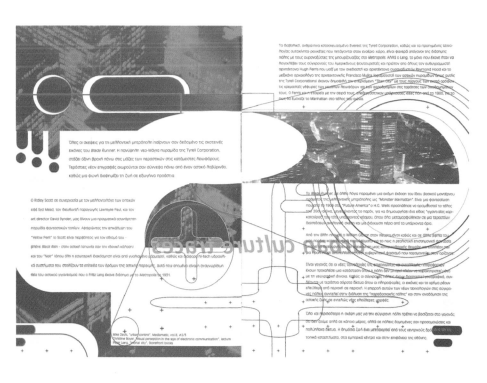

Trace Urban Culture Magazine

Greece 1996 Magazine 雑誌
CD: Tasos Efremidis
AD: Dimitris Mitsiopoulos
D: Apostolos Rizos / Klimis Mastoridis
DF: alterVision
CL: Self publication

Shift!-Heat Issue

Germany 1996　Magazine　雑誌
CD, AD, D: Lilly Tomec / Anja Lutz
　　　　　　　 / Horst Libera
DF, CL: Shift! Magazine

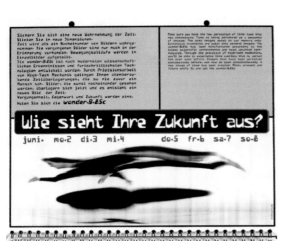

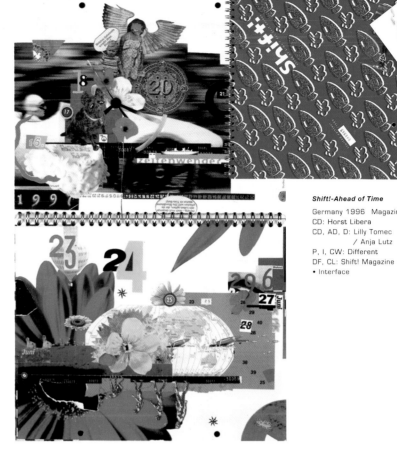

Shift!-Ahead of Time

Germany 1996 Magazine 雑誌
CD: Horst Libera
CD, AD, D: Lilly Tomec
/ Anja Lutz
P, I, CW: Different
DF, CL: Shift! Magazine
• Interface

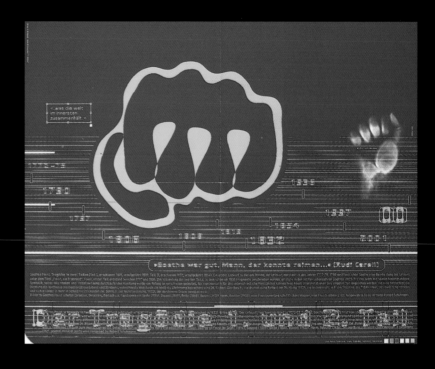

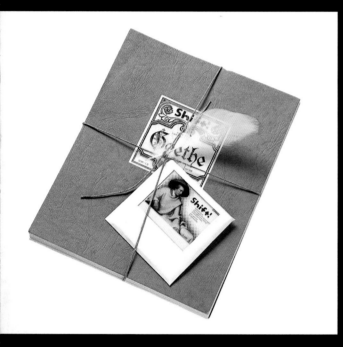

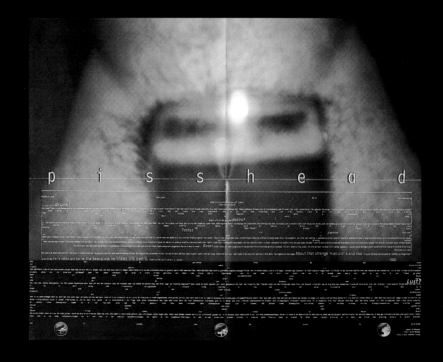

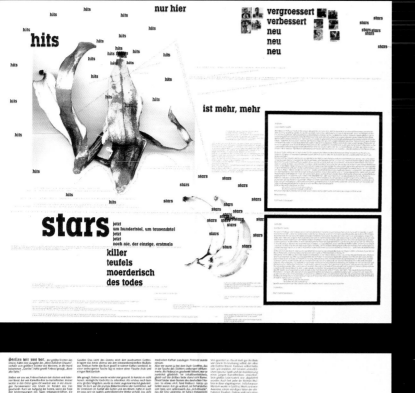

Shift!-Goethe

Germany 1997 Magazine 雑誌
CD: Horst Libera
CD, AD, D: Lilly Tomec / Anja Lutz
P, I, CW: Different
DF, CL: Shift! Magazine
• Interface, Lubalin, Ocr, Oaz X-Ray, etc.

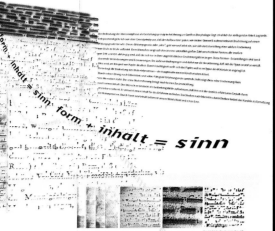

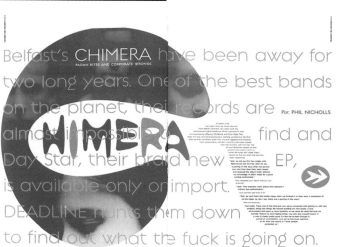

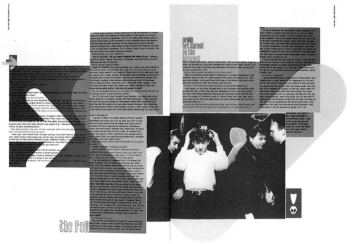

Deadline Magazine

UK 1995 Magazine 雜誌
CD, AD, D: Rian Hughes
DF: Device
CL: Deadline Magazine
Typeface Design: Darkside by Rian Hughes
• Amorpheus, Paradigm, Darkside, Elektron

it's new
It's nasty
but it's not >>>>>>>>>>

summer.1996

Garbage

66

la bana l vida

AUGUST 1996

It's New
It's Nasty
It's Not
Your Father's
Magazine

$6.99

Sana, sana, coulito de rana, que no sana hoy, sana mañana. Sana, sana, coulito de rana, que no sana hoy, sana mañana. Sana, sana, coulito de rana, que no sana hoy, sana mañana. Sana, sana, coulito de rana, que no sana hoy, sana mañana. Sana, sana, coulito de rana, que no sana hoy, sana mañana. Sana, sana, coulito de rana, que no sana hoy, sana mañana. Sana, sana, coulito de rana, que no sana hoy, sana mañana. Sana, sana, coulito de rana, que no sana hoy, sana mañana. sana, sana,

1. *Rage Box*

USA 1997 Press kit (box) 箱入りプレスキット
CD, AD: Mike Salisbury
D: Mary Evelyn McGough
P: Aaron Chans / others
CW: Bruce David / Larry Wichman
DF: Mike Salisbury Communications Inc.
CL: Rage Magazine
• Emigre

2. *Rage Magazine*

USA 1997 Magazine 雑誌
CD, AD, D: Mike Salisbury
D: Mary Evelyn McGough / Mick Haggerty
  / Will Evans
I: Margo Chase / others
DF: Mike Salisbury Communications Inc.
CL: Rage Magazine

See Molly at work.
She is doing all the things
that Wally is trying to do.
Only she does them better.

Molly has an Adaptec host
adapter and SCSI peripherals.
See Molly multitask. From her
PC to peripherals, and even to
her network, she really works fast!

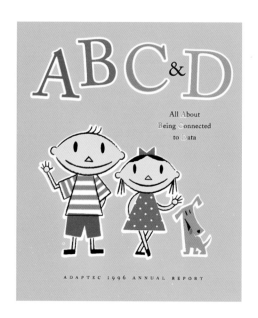

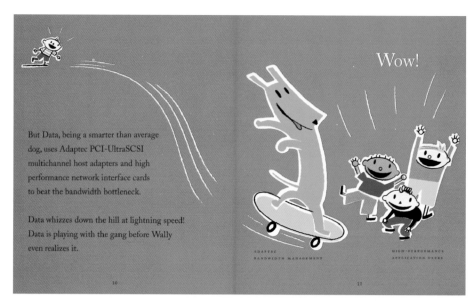

But Data, being a smarter than average
dog, uses Adaptec PCI-UltraSCSI
multichannel host adapters and high
performance network interface cards
to beat the bandwidth bottleneck.

Data whizzes down the hill at lightning speed!
Data is playing with the gang before Wally
even realizes it.

Wow!

No problem! Molly can configure her laptop with
Adaptec's PCMCIA host adapter and EZ-SCSI
software. And that will connect her with all kinds
of peripherals. Now Molly can do research on the
Internet, share files, make faxes and save her
homework from anywhere! Even from Space!

Adaptec 1996 Annual Report

USA 1996 Annual report アニュアルレポート
CD, AD: Bill Cahan
D, CW: Kevin Roberson
I: Richard McGuire
CW: Lindsay Beaman
DF: Cahan + Associates
CL: Adaptec
• Caslon

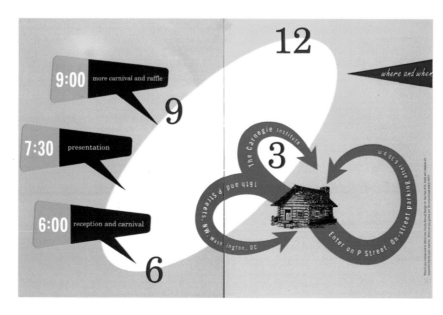

24 Hour Fun

USA 1996　Brochure　ブローシャ
CD, D, I: Melinda Beck
CW: Jennifer Kornegay / Paul Geary
DF: Melinda Beck Studio
CL: American Institute of Graphic Arts
• Hand-drawn type, Trixie, News Gothic,
Black Oak, Century Schoolbook,
Free Style Script

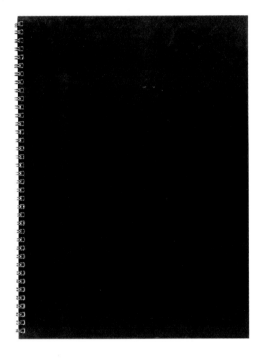

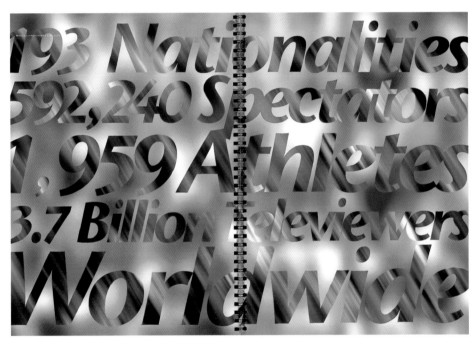

World Athletic Series

USA 1996 Brochure ブローシャ
CD, AD, D: Joel Fuller
AD, D: Todd Houser
D: Mike Lopez
CW: Frank Cunningham
DF: Pinkhaus
CL: International Amateur Athletic Federation
• Wunderlich

1. *Werkstattprogramm*

Switzerland 1997 Brochure ブローシャ
D: Thomas Bruggisser
DF: Grafiktraktor
CL: Daniela Winkler

2. *Texas Monthly*

USA 1996 Magazine spread 雑誌
CD: DJ Stout
D: Kathleen Marcus
I, Typography: Melinda Beck
CW: Helen Thorpe
CL: Texas Monthly
• Hand-drawn type

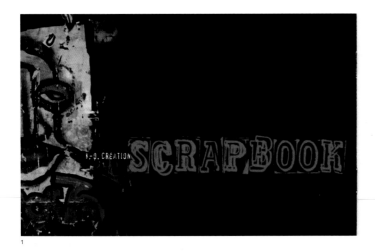

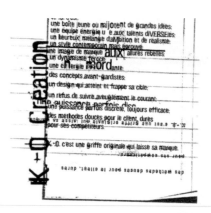

1

1. *Scrapbook*

Canada 1997
Brochure (Self promotion) ブローシャ
AD, D: Pol Baril / Denis Dulude
CW: Marie-Frédérique Laberge-Milot
DF, CL: K.-O. Création
• 2Rebels, [T-26], FontFont

2. *Marcus Struzina Photography - Booklet*

Australia 1997 Booklet ブックレット
AD, D: Andrew Hoyne
P: Marcus Struzina
CW: Greg
DF: Andrew Hoyne Design
CL: Marcus Struzina Photography
• Mr. Struzina

2

People get up, come over to me.

To look at me?

At the route map, behind my head.

Not so fast. There must be a lot of pieces.

The lights go out.

On to emergency.

Then black.

Did the jumper jump or was he pushed?

They never report the jumpers.

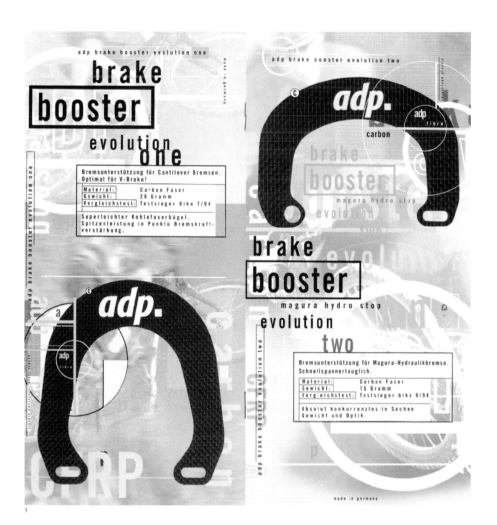

1. **ADP Product Catalogue**

Germany 1996 Catalog カタログ
CD, AD, D, I: Ruediger Goetz
DF: Simon & Goetz
CL: ADP Engineering GmbH
• Trade Gothic

2. **Heavy Handed**

Canada 1996
Promotional Booklet ブックレット
CD, AD, D: Noël Nanton
DF: Typotherapy + Design
CL: Whatnaut Records
• Custom Made, Diolog Dub,
  Board Game, Impact, Helvetica

PHYSIK

18.02.96 ... maison de radio france (festival présences). mauricio kagel - die stücke der windrose für salonorchester. mauricio kagel - dirigent

20.02.96 ... utrecht. muziekcentrum vredenburg. nederlandse ... programmastichting. mauricio kagel - die stücke der windrose für salonorchester. mauricio kagel - dirigent

21.02.96 ... metz. salle de l'arsenal. mauricio kagel - die stücke der windrose für salonorchester. mauricio kagel - dirigent

22.02.96 ... köln. philharmonie. mauricio kagel - die stücke der windrose für salonorchester. mauricio kagel - dirigent

23.02.96 ... düsseldorf. tonhalle. mauricio kagel - die stücke der windrose für salonorchester. mauricio kagel - dirigent

11. 01. 96 ... münchen. bayer... stadthalle. paul hindemith - kammermusik nr. 3. york höller - pas de deux für violoncello und klavier. györgy ligeti - konzert für violoncello und orchester. arnold schönberg - fünf orchesterstücke op. 16 in der fassung für kammerorchester. felix greissle. siegfried palm - violoncello und moderation. braxton blake - dirigent

23. 01. 96 ... köln. hochschule für musik. james tenney - water in the mountain... fire in heaven für e-git. und tonband. horst... joachim hespos - pinogó-tibun-i für tuba und kontrabaß. nicolaus a. huber - ohne hölderlin für kontrabaß und klavier. melvyn poore - lyric drum für e-gitarre, e-tuba und live-elektronik.

26. 01. 96 ... köln. orangerie schloß benrath. james tenney - water in the mountain... fire in heaven für e-git. und tonband. horst joachim hespos - pinogó-tibun-i für tuba und kontrabaß. nicolaus a. huber - ohne hölderlin für kontrabaß und klavier. melvyn poore - lyric drum für e-gitarre, e-tuba und live-elektronik.

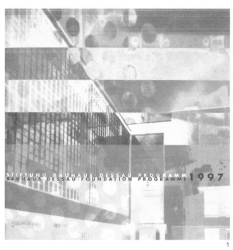

1

1. *Programme 1997*

Germany 1996 Brochure ブローシャ
D: Daniela Haufe / Sophie Alex
/ Detlef Fiedler
CW, DF: Cyan
CL: Bauhaus Dessau Foundation
• Futura

2. *Bauhaus 1919-1933*

Germany 1996 Brochure ブローシャ
D: Daniela Haufe / Sophie Alex
/ Detlef Fiedler
CW, DF: Cyan
CL: Bauhaus Dessau Foundation
• Futura

2

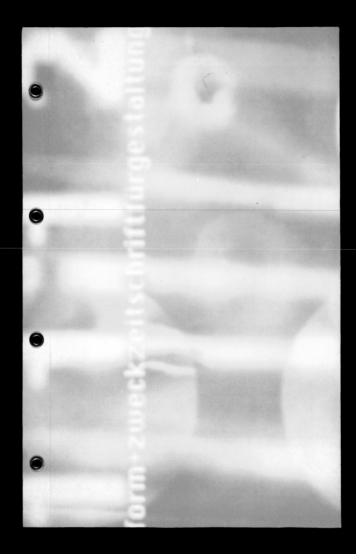

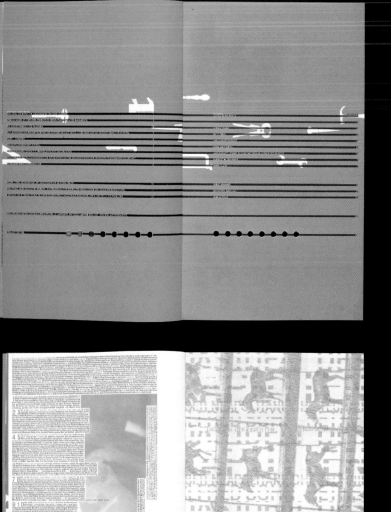

Form + Zweck 11/12

Germany 1995 Magazine 雑誌
D: Daniela Haufe / Sophie Alex
 / Detlef Fiedler
CW, DF: Cyan
CL: Form + Zweck
• Bureau Grotesk

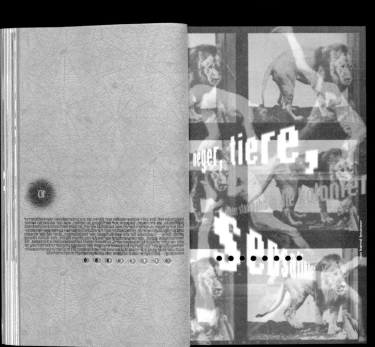

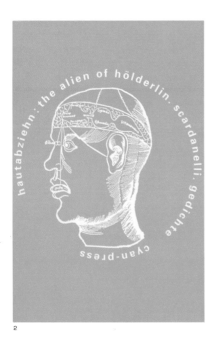

1. *Form + Zweck 9/10*

Germany 1994 Magazine 雑誌
D: Daniela Haufe / Sophie Alex
 / Detlef Fiedler
CW, DF: Cyan
CL: Form + Zweck
• Bureau Grotesk

2. *Scardanelli. Gedichte. Hautabziehn.*
The Aliens of Hölderlin.

Germany 1996 Publication 書籍
D: Daniela Haufe / Sophie Alex
 / Detlef Fiedler
CW, DF: Cyan
CL: Cyan Press
• Univers (Adobe)

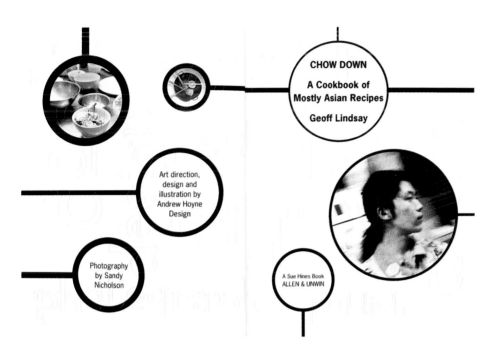

CHOW DOWN

A Cookbook of
Mostly Asian Recipes

Geoff Lindsay

Art direction, design and illustration by Andrew Hoyne Design

Photography by Sandy Nicholson

A Sue Hines Book
ALLEN & UNWIN

WOK BRUSHES for keeping the wok clean. Never use detergent on your wok. Wash it with hot water and a wok brush.

JAPANESE MANDOLINE for fine slicing, shredding, julienne and chip-making. Very sharp. Have the band-aids ready.

WOK, the most versatile cooking implement. Choose a steel wok. Season it by heating one tablespoon of peanut oil to smoking point. Wipe the surface of the wok with kitchen paper. Allow it to cool and repeat the process. The wok is then ready for use. Teflon woks are for nerds.

A Cookbook of Mostly Asian Recipes

CHOW DOWN

Geoff Lindsay

hot

Chow Down

Australia 1997 Publication 書籍
CD, AD, D: Andrew Hoyne
D: Rachel Miles
P: Sandy Nicholson
I: Mik Young Kim
CW: Geoff Lindsay
DF: Andrew Hoyne Design
CL: Allen & Unwin
• Mr. Chow

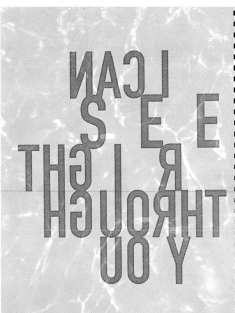

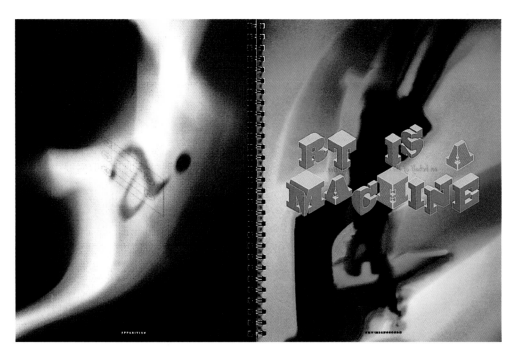

...I HEAR IT IN MY HEAD,

SO QUIET THAT WHEN I CONCENTRATE ON IT

THE NOISE IS **DEAFENING**.

SNATCHES OF WORDS, SPOKEN LANGUAGES,

THE SOUND OF GENERATIONS, OVERTONES THAT

TRICK THE SENSES.

PEOPLE LOOK AT YOU

THERE IS NO AVOIDING IT.

THE LUSTFUL EYES OF LIZARD-LIKE LOTHARIOS

OR THE CRITICAL **S T A R E**

OF SOMEONE'S MAIDEN AUNT.

I KNOW THEY WONDER **WHAT** I'M DOING THERE,

WITH THEM.

THEY WANT TO **LABEL** ME—

I GUESS IT'S ALL PART OF IT...

THE SNEAKING SUSPICION THAT **I MAY JUST**

BE PRETENDING.

THERE'S A FINE LINE BETWEEN MAKE-UP AND WAR PAINT...

Insights on Gildear

USA 1997 Brochure ブローシャ
CD, D, CW, DF: Thirst
P: Rick Valicenti / Wm. Valicenti
 / Chester
I: Deborah Ross (Water Color)
 / Patricking
CL: Gilbert Paper
• Thirstype's collection

INSIGHTS HAPPEN when you're walking through a familiar neighborhood & absentmindedness or curiosity takes you down a new street. A CHILL of DISORIENTATION.

Suddenly you stumble into another neighborhood that you know well.

You're not lost after all.

[Z]00 agenda 1996

The Netherlands 1995　Agenda ダイヤリー
CD, AD, D: Ben Faydherbe
D: Wout de Vringer
CW: Gerrit Willems
DF: Faydherbe / De Vringer
CL: [Z]00-Productions
• Collossalis, Trixie, Shelley Script

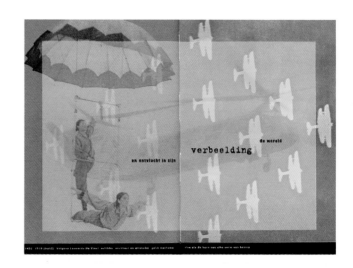

ESSE

USA 1997 Brochure ブローシャ
CD, D, CW, DF: Thirst
P: Rick Valicenti / Wm. Valicenti
 / Chester
I: Deborah Ross (Water Color)
 / Patricking
CL: Gilbert Paper
• Thirstype's collection

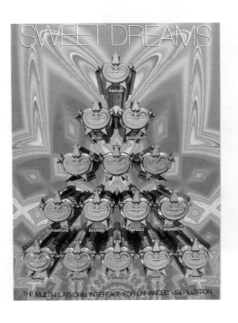

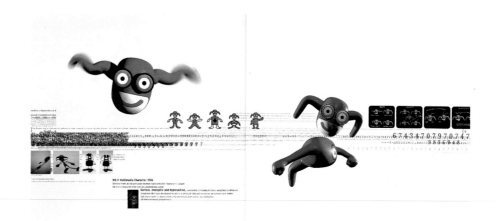

Nofrontiere Operating System

Austria 1996 Publication 書籍
CD, AD, D: Andrea Steinfl
D: Christine Zmölnig
D(★): Anja Albersmeier / Mark Lycette
　　 / Anja Weißbacher
3D Modeling(Mr.V): Giancarlo Lari
CW: Morgan Russell / Tiziana Panizza
CL: Nofrontiere Design GmbH
• Mrs Eaves, Interstate

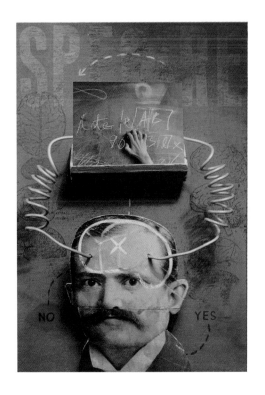

MAYBE GOOD DESIGN
ISN'T PRETTY

FIGURING OUT WHAT
DRIVES PEOPLE CRAZY

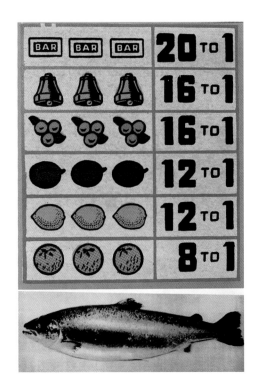

IF IT WAS SIMPLY A
MATTER OF PLAYING
THE ODDS, YOU MIGHT
CONSIDER HATCHING SALMON,
OR, FOR THAT MATTER,
YOU MIGHT AS WELL BUY A LOTTERY TICKET.
IT'S EASIER

CHANCES THAT
THERE IS LIFE ON
ANOTHER PLANET
1 IN 1,000,000,000

1. *Maybe Good Design Isn't Pretty*

USA 1996 Brochure ブローシャ
CD, AD: Bill Cahan
D: Bob Dinetz
CW: Danny Altman
DF: Cahan + Associates
CL: GVO

2. *Chances That There Is Life...*

USA 1996 Brochure ブローシャ
CD, AD: Bill Cahan
D, I: Bob Dinetz
I: Gary Baseman
CW: Stefanie Marlis
DF: Cahan + Associates
CL: GVO

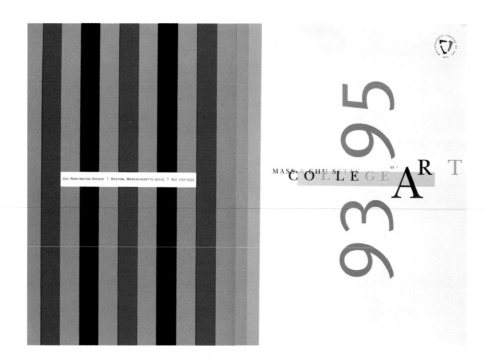

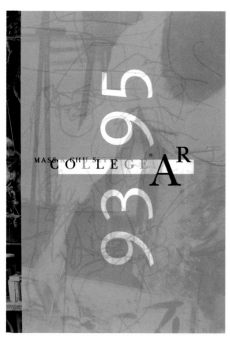

Massachusetts College of Art Catalog

USA 1993 Catalog カタログ
CD, AD, D: Clifford Stoltze
D: Kyong Choe / Peter Farrell
 / Rebecca Fagan
DF: Stoltze Design
CL: Massachusetts College of Art
• Meta, New Baskerville, Trixie

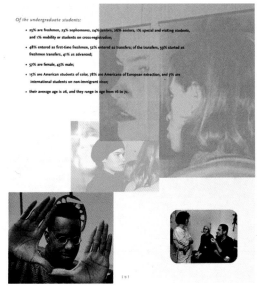

Massachusetts College of Art Catalog
95/97

USA 1995 Catalog カタログ
AD, D: Clifford Stoltze
D: Tracy Schroeder / Heather Kramer
 / Peter Farrell / Resa Blatman
P: Cecilia Hirsch / Jon Baring-Gould
CW: Elizabeth Mackie
DF: Stoltze Design
CL: Massachusetts College of Art

1. Performance Art Festival 1996

USA 1996 Brochure ブローシャ
D, I: Mark Murphy
I: Brian Fristik
CW: Thomas Mulready
DF: Murphy Design, Inc.
CL: Performance Art Festival
• Clique Wedge, Odeon, Goudy

2. AGFA Type Idea Catalog

USA 1995 Catalog カタログ
CD. AD, D: Carlos Segura
D: Brenda Rotheiser
DF: Segura Inc.
CL: AGFA

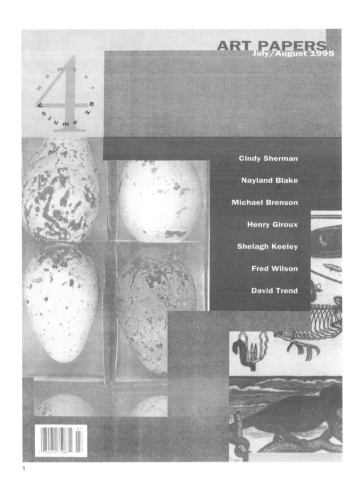

1

2

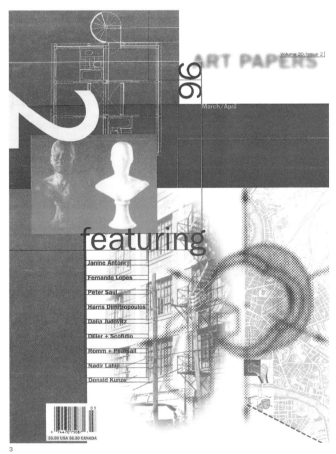

3

4

1,2,3. **Art Papers**

USA 1995(1)/1996(2,3) Magazine 雑誌
CD, AD, D: Pattie Belle Hastings
AD, D: Bjorn Akselsen
DF: Icehouse Design, Atlanta and New Haven
CL: Atlanta Art Papers Inc.
• Franklin Gothic, New Century Schoolbook

4. **Ars Musica**

Belgium 1996/97 Brochure ブローシャ
AD, D: Jean-Marc Klinkert / Oliver Lamy
P: Rodney Graham
DF: NSD
CL: Ars Musica
• News Gothic, Sabon

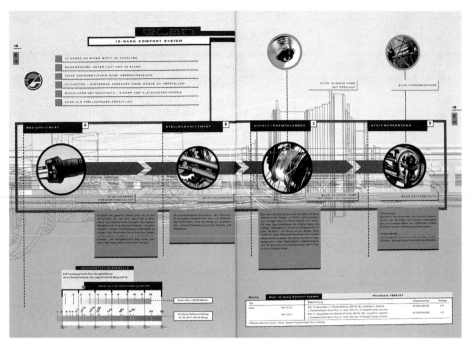

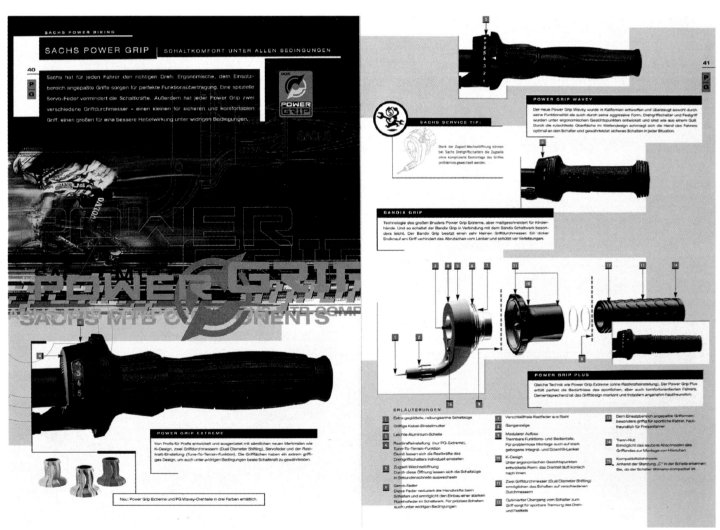

Sachs Product Catalogue 1997

Germany 1996 Catalog カタログ
CD, AD, D: Ruediger Goetz
D, I: Christian Dekant
I: Manuela Schmidt
DF: Simon & Goetz
CL: Fichtel & Sachs AG
• Helvetica

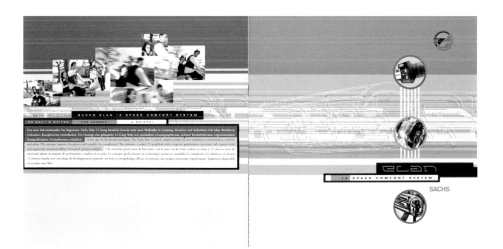

1. **Sachs Elan Folder**

Germany 1996 Brochure ブローシャ
CD, D: Ruediger Goetz
AD, D: Christian Dekant
P: Rui Camillo
I: Manuela Schmidt
CW: M. Gressner
DF: Simon & Goetz
CL: Fichtel & Sachs AG
• Helvetica

2. **Sachs MTB Advertisement**

Germany 1996 Advertisement 広告物
CD, AD, D: Ruediger Goetz
D, I: Christian Dekant
I: Manuela Schmidt
CW: Stefan Freier
DF: Simon & Goetz
CL: Fichtel & Sachs AG
• Helvetica

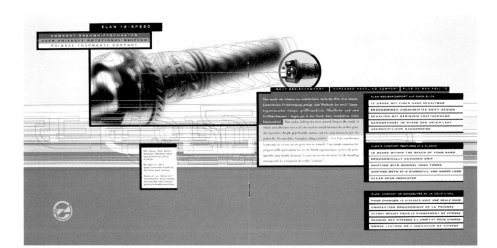

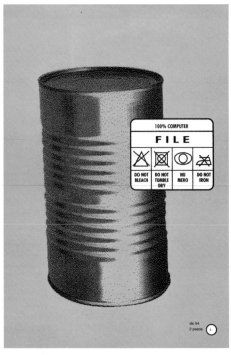

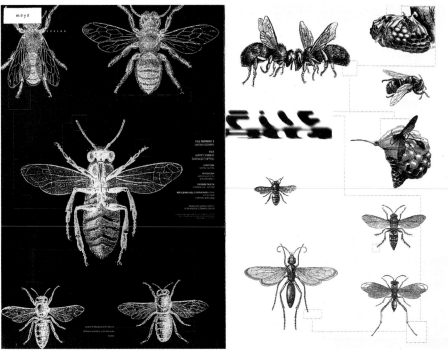

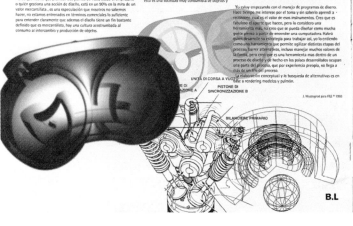

File Numero 3

Argentina 1994   Magazine 雑誌
CD, AD, D: Santiago Felippelli
/ Andrés Sobrino
DF: Bridger Conway Ag
• Helvetica, Futura

Programme Polymachina

France 1997 Brochure ブローシャ
CD, AD, D: Jean-Jacques Tachdjian
DF: i comme image
CL: L'Aeronef
• Alterna, Alex, Nobody,
  Centauri (Radiateur® fontes)

Come on, let's play something.
Okay. Catching? Hide and seek? Police catch thief?
Nope. Let's do something different this time.
Like what? Chatek? Pepsi-cola one-two-three?
Let's meet tonight. Bring some papers and matches.
What are we going to do?
It's Showtime!

Feeling nostalgic, I am walking down memory lane, trying to recollect my childhood. Do join me.

Grandma's praying again!

Why are all things so big and tall?

It happened one night when my friends and I decided to see some real fire in action. We gathered papers to burn in a drain. The fire grew bigger and stronger than we had expected. Panicked, we ran home to get pails of water and managed to put the fire out. No adult knew about this at all.

The patterns on the window grills just remind me of delicious beans....yum yum....

"Finish your food, or the policeman is coming to catch you."

Adults always like to say things to scare children who are disobedient. I remember grandma used to scare me with words like "either the officer or bad guy will come and take you away" whenever I refused to take a shower or finish my food.

REMEMBER

HAVE A NICE DAY

Peep Show

Singapore 1996 Catalog カタログ
D: Andrew Dallas Naylor / Lee Huei Peng
  / Paul Van Der Veer
CW: Jeri Suryani Tosripin
DF: Epigram
CL: Peep Show
• Meta, Warehouse, Oblong, Basket Case

which one is for the fan?
which one is for the light?

Kitchen - so near yet so far....

My friends and I enjoyed playing games and looking out for new adventures. One thing we never failed to do was to make the adults worry for us when we refused to go home. Then, the grand finale came whenever grandpa brought a cane along with him and chased us to go home. We dispersed within seconds.

REMINISCING

what shall we play today?

Where's Dong-dong-chiang? He's supposed to bring the racket to play badminton.

How about masak-masak like the rocketman?

Cheeh-ko-pa?

Scissors-paper-stone?

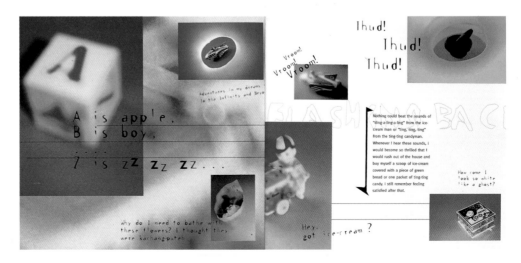

A is apple,
B is boy.
Z is zZ zZ zZ...

Adventures in my dreams to the infinity and beyond

Vroom! Vroom! Vroom!

Thud! Thud! Thud!

FLASHING BACK

Nothing could beat the sounds of "ding-a-ling-a-ling" from the ice-cream man or "ting, ting, ting" from the ting-ting candyman. Whenever I hear these sounds, I would become so thrilled that I would rush out of the house and buy myself a scoop of ice-cream covered with a piece of green bread or one packet of ting-ting candy. I still remember feeling satisfied after that.

How come I look so white like a ghost?

why do I need to bathe with these flowers? I thought they were kachang-puteh.

Hey, got ice-cream?

142

1. **Connection 4**

France 1995 Brochure ブローシャ
CD, AD, D: Sébastien Dragon
        / Simon Clarck
AD: Philippe Starcu
CL: Thomson (Multi Media)
• Univers, Home made typeface

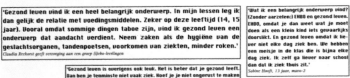

Onderwerpen
voor verzorging in de basisvorming

s l o

2. **De Keuze is aan U.**

The Netherlands Pamphlet パンフレット
D, I: Karin Nefs
CW: Mick Hansen
DF: Proforma, Amersfoort
CL: S. L. O.

'Gezond leven vind ik een heel belangrijk onderwerp. In mijn lessen leg ik dan gelijk de relatie met voedingsmiddelen. Zeker op deze leeftijd (14, 15 jaar). Vooral omdat sommige dingen taboe zijn, vind ik gezond leven een onderwerp dat aandacht verdient. Neem zaken als de hygiëne van de geslachtsorganen, tandenpoetsen, voorkomen van ziekten, minder roken.'
Claudia Reckorst geeft verzorging aan een groep lfjbrho-leerlingen

'Wat ik een belangrijk onderwerp vind? (Zonder aarzelen:) EHBO en gezond leven. EHBO, omdat je dan weet wat je moet doen als een klein kind iets gevaarlijks doorslikt. En gezond leven omdat ik liever niet elke dag ziek ben. We hebben een meisje in de klas die is bijna elke dag ziek. Ik zelf ga liever naar school dan dat ik ziek thuis zit.'
Sabine Hooft, 13 jaar, mavo-2

'Voeding vind ik ook de aandacht waard. Niet alleen meiden, maar ook jongens moeten weten hoe ze verpakkingsetiketten kunnen lezen. Je staat er overigens verbaasd van hoe geïnteresseerd jongens zijn in de vetten die in voedsel zitten. (Lachend:) de lijn is bij hen net zo goed een onderwerp dat volop belangstelling wekt.'
Mary Klumpers, docent Verzorging aan het Pasculcollege (mavo, havo, vwo)

'Koken vind ik het leukst. Je leert ervan. Thuis kook ik nog niet.'
Soumaya Bouchouihan, 14 jaar Ifjrbo

'Gezond leven is overigens ook leuk. Het is beter dat je gezond leeft. Dan ben je tenminste niet vaak ziek. Hoef je je niet ongerust te maken dat je iets hebt. Wat gezond leven inhoudt? Nou eh, je elke dag douchen, niet roken, dan heb je namelijk weinig kans op kanker. En dat je niet te veel, maar ook niet te weinig eet. Oh ja, en bewegen...'
Jarmo Dokkum, 14 jaar, mavo-2

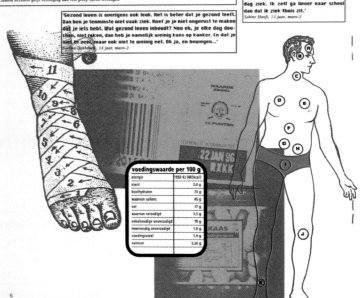

voedingswaarde per 100 g	
energie	1950 KJ (465kcal)
eiwit	5,0 g
koolhydraten	73 g
waarvan suikers	45 g
vet	17 g
waarvan verzadigd	5,5 g
enkelvoudig onverzadigd	10 g
meervoudig onverzadigd	1,0 g
voedingsvezel	1,9 g
natrium	0,26 g

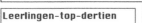

Leerlingen-top-dertien

1. Gezond leven
2. Genotmiddelen
3. Puberteit
4. EHBO
5. Voeding
6. Relaties
7. Milieu
8. Financiën
9. Groepen
10. Kleding
11. Werk en ontspanning
12. Zorg
13. Wonen

'Wat ik echt een heel belangrijk onderwerp vind? Kinderverzorging. Gewoon omdat het leuk is. Bejaarden vind ik niet zo leuk. Dat gaat namelijk over verschonen.'
Aawaina Joval, 15 jaar Ifjrbo

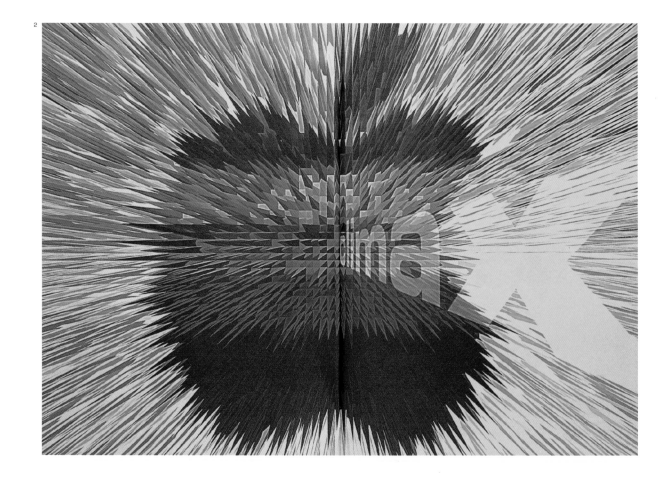

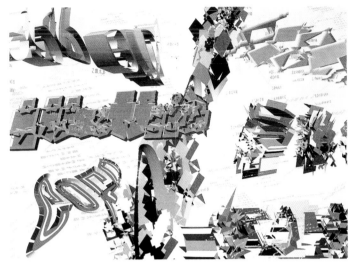

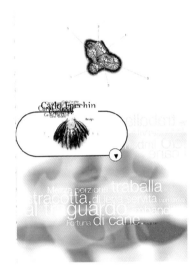

1. *Creative Impulse 5*

Italy 1997   Publication 書籍
CD: Fabio Caleffi / Dina Cucchiaro
AD, D, CW: Art Force
P: Roberto Ricci
I: Marco Papazzoni
CL, Publisher: Happy Books

2. *Climax 03 - 20x20, Climax vs Apple*

Italy 1997   Magazine 雑誌
CD, AD, D: A.Jumbo Manfredini
              / Giorgio Cantadori
CW: Dina Cucchiaro / Alessio Leonardi
CL: Apple Computers
Publisher: Happy Books

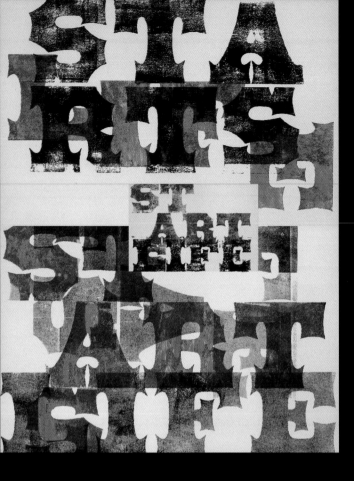

The Alternative Pick

USA 1996   Campaign キャンペーン
CD, AD, D, I: Carlos Segura
I: Hatch
DF: Segura Inc.
CL: The Alternative Pick
• Boxspring, Mattress

The Alternative Pick

USA 1996   Campaign キャンペーン
CD, AD, D, I: Carlos Segura
I: Hatch
DF: Segura Inc.
CL: The Alternative Pick
• Boxspring, Mattress

"I was inspired by music — the rich colors, the creativity and the fluidity. And I knew that in designing a music museum, I needed to reach out to that constituency of music lovers — wherever they may be."

With those words, EMP architect Frank Gehry unveiled the schematic design of Experience Music Project's 110,000-square-foot museum, scheduled to open at Seattle Center in 1999. The design — Gehry and EMP's shared vision of the museum's home — combines six diverse elements that will potentially be crafted from a variety of materials including tomato, stainless steel, plaster and even glass tiles. The rich colors — hues of red, blue, gold, yellow and white — were inspired by electric guitars, and at this stage are meant to fuel discussions about final color ideas.

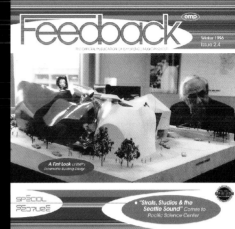

Feedback

emp

THE OFFICIAL PUBLICATION OF EXPERIENCE MUSIC PROJECT

Winter 1996
Issue 2.4

A First Look at EMP's Schematic Building Design

SPECIAL FEATURES

• "*Strats, Studios & the Seattle Sound*" Comes to Pacific Science Center

---

Questions & Answers
with the Curators
Go ahead - ask anything you want!

QUESTIONS?
Send them to our curators at:
EXPERIENCE MUSIC PROJECT
PO Box 45460
Seattle, WA 98145
e-mail:
feedback@experience.org

q: Will Experience Music Project be online? Will I be able to take a tour of the museum from my computer, or will I have to "physically" stop by when the museum is open?
-Lisa Holt, lisah@arkspace.com

a: Great question Lisa! Experience Music Project will be interactive in many ways, including taking advantage of the World Wide Web. Right now you can visit us online at http://www.experience.org. Over the Web visitors can learn more about the project, take a virtual tour of our artifact vault with a curator, meet our architect or e-mail us questions about anything and everything. Starting in 1997, we'll significantly enhance our Web site to include even more cool interactive experiences, and by the time we open in 1999 you'll be able to browse our huge collection of rock 'n' roll artifacts online and make some music of your own.

q: I saw a picture of EMP's schematic building design in the paper and wonder what was the inspiration behind the design?
-Angela Newlove, angelan@wagged.com

a: Our architect Frank Gehry took his inspiration from music and musical instruments - the building has a real ephemeral, fluid shape to it - some even call it swoopy! The colors are inspired by the rich variety of colors you see on electric guitars, and although the color concepts will continue to evolve before we open, you can bet that Frank will continue to draw from the creativity in music.

q: Who was the first Northwest musician to achieve notoriety?
-Lora Loftis, lloftis@aol.com

a: It seems that the earliest musician from the Pacific Northwest to have achieved an international reputation was Olympia's Theo Karle (Johnston). Born in 1893, Karle had earned a reputation as a fine up-and-coming young tenor singer by age 16. By 1918 he had sung in New York and with the Seattle Philharmonic Orchestra. Over the next few years he recorded many records for top labels (and obscure Seattle firms) and toured throughout Europe. In 1930 he began eight years of broadcasting his own radio show on CBS. He passed away at his home in Seattle in 1972.

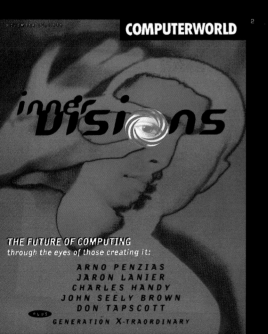

COMPUTERWORLD

inner visions

THE FUTURE OF COMPUTING
through the eyes of those creating it:

ARNO PENZIAS
JARON LANIER
CHARLES HANDY
JOHN SEELY BROWN
DON TAPSCOTT
PLUS
GENERATION X-TRAORDINARY

1. *Feed Back 2.4*

USA 1996 Newsletter ニュースレター
CD: Jason Hunke
AD: Modern Dog
D, I: Vittorio Costarella / Robynne Raye
P: Lara Swimmer / Joshua White
DF: Modern Dog
CL: Experience Music Project
• Avant Garde, Euphoric

2. *Innervisions*

USA 1996 Magazine 雑誌
CD, AD, D: Clifford Stoltze
D: Wing Ip Ngan
P(cover): Craig MacCormack
I: Joe Polevy
DF: Stoltze Design
CL: Computer World
• Cyberotica, Truth

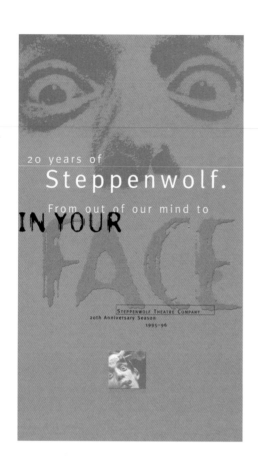

20 years of
Steppenwolf.

From out of our mind to

IN YOUR

FACE

STEPPENWOLF THEATRE COMPANY
20th Anniversary Season
1995-96

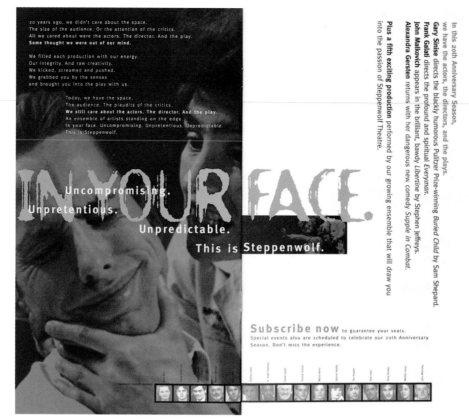

20 years ago, we didn't care about the space.
The size of the audience. Or the attention of the critics.
All we cared about were the actors. The director. And the play.
Some thought we were out of our mind.

We filled each production with our energy.
Our integrity. And raw creativity.
We kicked, screamed and pushed.
We grabbed you by the senses
and brought you into the play with us.

Today, we have the space.
The audience. The plaudits of the critics.
We still care about the actors. The director. And the play.
An ensemble of artists standing on the edge.
In your face. Uncompromising. Unpretentious. Unpredictable.
This is Steppenwolf.

In this 20th Anniversary Season,
we have the actors, the directors, and the plays.
Gary Sinise directs the blackly humorous Pulitzer Prize-winning *Buried Child* by Sam Shepard.
Frank Galati directs the profound and spiritual *Everyman*.
John Malkovich appears in the brilliant, bawdy *Libertine* by Stephen Jeffreys.
Alexandra Gersten returns with her dangerous new comedy *Supple in Combat*.

Plus a fifth exciting production performed by our growing ensemble that will draw you
into the passion of Steppenwolf Theatre.

IN YOUR FACE.

Uncompromising.
Unpretentious.
Unpredictable.
This is Steppenwolf.

Subscribe now to guarantee your seats.
Special events also are scheduled to celebrate our 20th Anniversary
Season. Don't miss the experience.

Steppenwolf 1995/1996 Season Brochure

USA 1995 Brochure ブローシャ
CD, AD: Mark Oldach
D: Mark Meyer
CW: Linda Chryle
DF: Mark Oldach Design
CL: Steppenwolf Theater Company
• Meta, Reactor

Dear Steppenwolf Supporter,

As Steppenwolf Theatre Company approaches its 20th
Anniversary Season, we are proud of our tremendous growth,
enhanced by your support, which has brought Steppenwolf
to a level where we can pursue our artistic goals with even
greater resources. Looking forward to our future, we are
excited by all of the challenging artistic opportunities afforded
by the talents of our ensemble.

Martha Lavey, Acting Artistic Director

To ensure that our 20th Anniversary Season is our most successful
ever, we are counting on you to continue your tradition of support.
Because ticket sales cover only 68% of our operating expenses—
including actors' salaries and production costs—Steppenwolf
productions are only possible with your generous support.

Gary Fencik, Chairman, 20th Anniversary Season

When you subscribe to Steppenwolf today, we hope you will
include a tax-deductible contribution in honor of our 20th
Anniversary. In addition to supporting our artistic programs,
your contribution will entitle you to many exclusive benefits.

Gary Sinise, Co-Chairman, 20th Anniversary Season

Thank you in advance for your ongoing support
which will enable Steppenwolf to soar to even greater
artistic heights during our 20th Anniversary Season.

p.s.
Join the Director's Circle.
For a donation of $1,500 you can join
our Directors Circle and receive two
complimentary subscriptions. For more
information, call Judith Simons, Director
of Development, at 312/335-1888.

Steppenwolf Theatre Company gratefully acknowledges the following sponsors of our 20th Anniversary Season:
Grand Benefactor   Premier Benefactor   Distinguished Benefactor

CITIBANK   **Sprint**   **UNITED AIRLINES**
Chicago's Hometown Airline

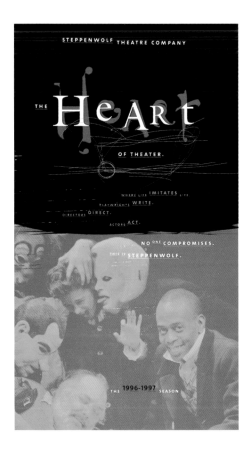

Steppenwolf 1996/1997 Season Brochure

USA 1996 Brochure ブローシャ
CD: Mark Oldach
D: Guido Mendez
CW: Linda Chryle
DF: Mark Oldach Design
CL: Steppenwolf Theater Company
• Thesis

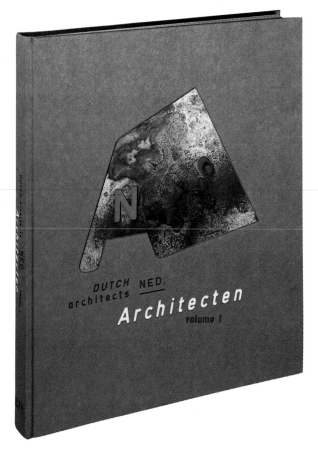

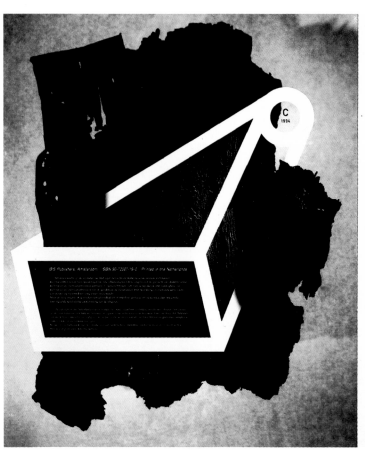

Dutch Architecture, Vol. 1

The Netherlands 1995 Publication 書籍
CD, AD, D: Jacques Koeweiden
      / Paul Postma
P: Marc van Praag
DF: Koeweiden Postma Associates
CW, CL: BIS Publishers
• KP Din

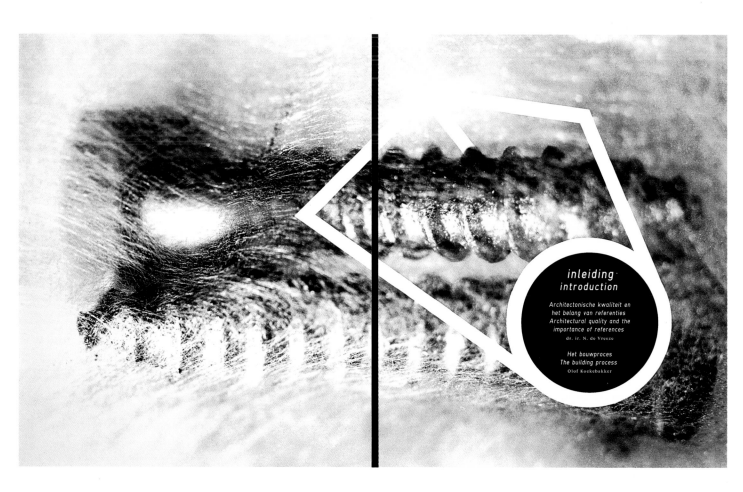

inleiding
introduction

Architectonische kwaliteit en
het belang van referenties
Architectural quality and the
importance of references
dr. ir. N. de Vreeze

Het bouwproces
The building process
Olof Koekebakker

register
index

23
Aardewerk Partners
Architekten & Ontwerpers BNA BNI bNO
Prinses Mariestraat 13/a
2514 KC Den Haag
T. (070) 3646226
F. (070) 3561266

24
AAtW Architecten
Oostenburgervoorstraat 148
1018 MR Amsterdam
T. (020) 4200206
F. (020) 4202292

Opgericht / *Founded:* 1990
Aantal medewerkers / *Staff:* 3
Contactpersonen / *Contacts:* ir. Aletta van Aalst
BNA, ir. Adrie E.P. Barnhard, André Hillebrand

Bureauprofiel
De vaste kern bestaat uit twee architecten en een
bouwkundig projectleider, ieder met een onderling
sterk verschillende achtergrond. Ook als AAtW werken wij aan uiteenlopende projecten, waarbij voor
ons zowel het esthetische als het organisatorische
vakmanschap uitgangspunt blijft.

Projecten
Renovatie tot negen appartementen Stationsweg/
Kikkerstraat, Den Haag (1993), Eye-catcher Lens,
Arnhem (1992), renovatie twee woningen Dunne
Bierkade, Den Haag (1992), bedienings- en energie-
gebouw Nieuwe Oranjesluis, Amsterdam (1994),
bloemen- en plantenkiosk Hofzichtlaan, Den Haag
(1994), renovatie tien woningen Lekstraat, Den
Haag (1993), voormgevingadvies sluizencomplex
Nieuwe Oranjesluis, Amsterdam (1994), groot on-
derhoud woning en winkel Stationsweg, Den Haag
(1993), verbouw en inrichting kantoor Kalkhaven,
Gorinchem (1992), verbouw en inrichting kantoor
Jan van Nassaustraat, Den Haag (1992), verbouw
kantoor Nassaukaan, Den Haag (1992), Centrale
Post Scheepvaartdienst, Wijk bij Duurstede (1994),
verbouwing woning, Zuidwolde (Dr.) (1993), bedie-
ningsgebouw Grote Sluis, Vianen (1995).

Profile
*The permanent core consists of two architects and a
technical project leader, each with a strongly differing
background. As AAtW Architecten, we work on a
wide variety of projects. Our guiding principle is profes-
sionalism, both in aesthetic and organizational
respects.*

Projects
*Conversion to nine apartments, Stationsweg/ Kikker-
straat, The Hague (1993), Eye-catcher Lens, Arnhem
(1992), renovation of two dwellings, Dunne Bierkade,
The Hague (1992), control and power generation building, Nieuwe Oranjesluis, Amsterdam (1994), florist's
kiosk, Hofzichtlaan, The Hague (1994), renovation of
ten dwellings, Lekstraat, The Hague (1993), design consultation, Nieuwe Oranjesluis Locks, Amsterdam (1994),
major renovation of dwelling and shop, Stationsweg,
The Hague (1993), conversion and furnishing of office,
Kalkhaven, Gorinchem (1992), conversion and furnishing of office, Jan van Nassaustraat, The Hague (1992),
office conversion, Nassaukaan, The Hague (1992), design consultation, Waterways Service Central Post, Wijk*

bij Duurstede (1994), house conversion, Zuidwolde (Dr.)
(1993), Grote Sluis control building, Vianen (1995).

26
Abken bv
Newtonbaan 1
3439 NK Nieuwegein
T. (03402) 38584
F. (03402) 53802

Opgericht / *Founded:* september 1958
Aantal medewerkers / *Staff:* 11
Contactpersoon / *Contact:* J.A. van Egmond
Lidmaatschappen / *Memberships:* BNA, BNI
Prijzen / *Prizes:* diverse competitieplannen /
various prizes in competitions

Bureauprofiel
Het bureau is maatschap van drie architecten. Er
zijn totaal elf mensen werkzaam. Werkgebieden
omvatten woningbouw, huisvesting ouderen,
kantoren, bedrijfsgebouwen, recreatieve projecten,
kerken, sociaal-culturele ruimten, winkels, school-
gebouwen en stedebouwkundig werk. Ook buiten-
landse projecten, met name in Frankrijk.

Opdrachtgevers
Woningbouwverenigingen, gemeenten, overheid,
projectontwikkelingsmaatschappijen, aannemers,
beleggers, bedrijven en particulieren.

Profile
*The firm consists of a partnership of three architects.
Eleven people are employed. Fields of work include housing, accommodation for the elderly, offices, company
premises, recreational projects, churches, social/cultural
buildings, shops, schools and town planning/urban
design. International projects, especially in France.*

Clients
*Housing associations, municipalities, government, pro-
ject development companies, contractors, investors,
industry and private individuals.*

28
AG Nova Architecten BNA
Zuidvliet 26
8921 BL Leeuwarden
Postbus 856
8901 BR Leeuwarden
T. (058) 129941
F. (058) 129988

Hertog van Saxenlaan 76/b
8801 ET Franeker
Postbus 234
8800 AE Franeker
T. (05170) 96600
F. (05170) 95575

Daltonstraat 10
3817 VB Amersfoort
T. (033) 632454
F. (033) 637642

Opgericht / *Founded:* 1975
Aantal medewerkers / *Staff:* ± 40
Contactpersonen / *Contacts:* C. Slot BNA
(Leeuwarden), en ir. J. Bos BNA (Amersfoort)

Bureauprofiel
Het bureau, met vestigingen in Leeuwarden, Franeker en Amersfoort, heeft een langdurige ervaring in
het ontwerpen, begeleiden en adviseren van projecten op het gebied van woningbouw en utiliteits-
bouw. Met een enthousiast team van ca. veertig medewerkers worden werken gerealiseerd van een sterk
uiteenlopend karakter en een uitgesproken architectuur. De architectuur als beeldend middel van de
gebouwde omgeving staat bij ons centraal. Binnen
de bureauorganisatie is een ingenieursbureau opge-
nomen, dat ons in staat stelt de constructie een
geïntegreerd deel te laten zijn van het ontwerp.
Het tekenwerk wordt over het algemeen geautoma-
tiseerd uitgevoerd.

Directie: ir. J. Bos b.i., H. Hettema, W. Kok, C. Slot,
F.J. de Vos BNA, M.J. Klijnstra, ir. P.T. Brouwer c.i.

Gerealiseerde werken
O.a. woningbouw (Amersfoort Kattenbroek, Apeldoorn Woudhuis, Almere, Gorinchem, Hoofddorp
en Assen), kantoren (Utrecht, Groningen, Leeuwarden en Sneek), banken (Leeuwarden), horeca
(Amersfoort, Utrecht en Apeldoorn), winkelcentra
(Wolvega en Amersfoort), gezondheidszorg (tehuis
voor geestelijk gehandicapten in Drachten, Leeuwarden en Wolvega, tandartsenpraktijk in Barneveld en Amersfoort, fysiotherapie in Amersfoort),
onderwijs (HBO-complex in Leeuwarden en scholen
voor voortgezet en basisonderwijs op diverse loca-
ties, jongerencentrum in Amersfoort Kattenbroek),
renovatie/restauratie (bejaardentehuizen, landhui-
zen en kazernes), overige werken (atelier voor leder-
waren in Italië, sportschool in Amersfoort, diverse
industriële projecten, diverse projecten voor Dieren-
park Amersfoort).

Profile
*The firm, which has offices in Leeuwarden, Franeker
and Amersfoort, has extensive experience in designing,
managing and advising on projects in the fields of housing and utility building. With our enthusiastic team of
about forty members of staff, we carry out projects of a
widely varying character and with a pronounced architecture. One of our central concerns is the role of architecture as a visual means for the built environment. The
structure of our firm incorporates an engineering consul-
tancy that gives us the capacity to treat the construction
as an integral part of the design. The drawing work is
largely automated.*

Completed projects
*Include housing (Amersfoort Kattenbroek, Apeldoorn
Woudhuis, Almere, Gorinchem, Hoofddorp and Assen),
offices (Utrecht, Groningen, Leeuwarden and Sneek),
banks (Leeuwarden), hotels and catering (Amersfoort,
Utrecht and Apeldoorn), shopping centres (Wolvega and
Amersfoort), health care themes for mentally handicap-
ped persons in Drachten, Leeuwarden and Wolvega,
dental practices in Barneveld and Amersfoort, physio-
therapy practice in Amersfoort), education (tertiary education complex in Leeuwarden and schools for primary/
secondary education in various places, youth centre in
Amersfoort Kattenbroek), renovation/restoration (old-age
homes, country houses and military barracks), other
projects (studio for leather goods in Italy, sports school
in Amersfoort, various industrial projects, various
projects for Amersfoort Zoo).*

263

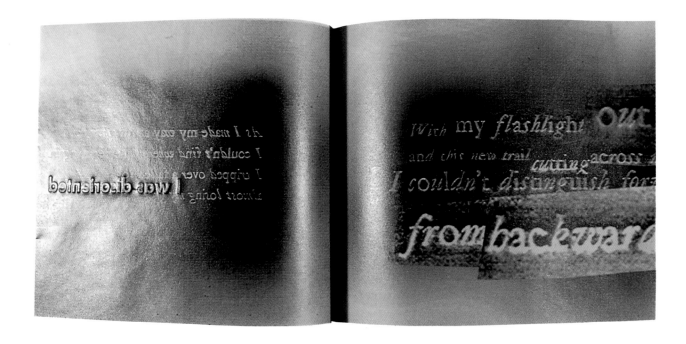

Henry

USA 1996 Publication 書籍
CD, AD, D, P, I, CW: Kari Strand
DF: Cranbrook Academy of Art
CL: Self-published
• Caslon, Futura
∗see p217

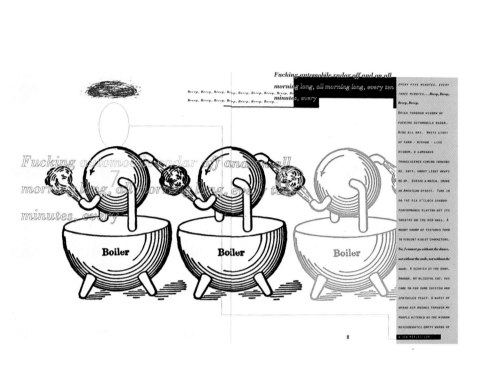

The Extended Moment

USA 1995 Magazine 雑誌
D, I: Daniel R. Smith
P, I, CW: Roderick Romero
DF: Command Z
CL: Self published
• Bodoni, Orator

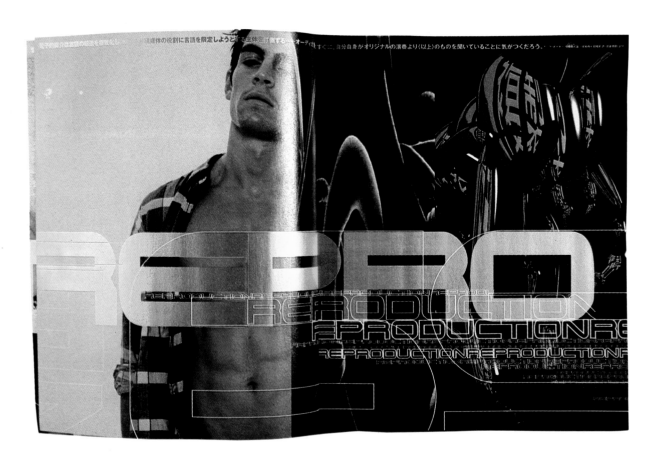

Wired Magazine

USA 1997 Magazine spreads 雑誌
CD, AD, D, P: Robert Bergman-Ungar
DF: Bergman-Ungar Associates
CL: Wired Magazine

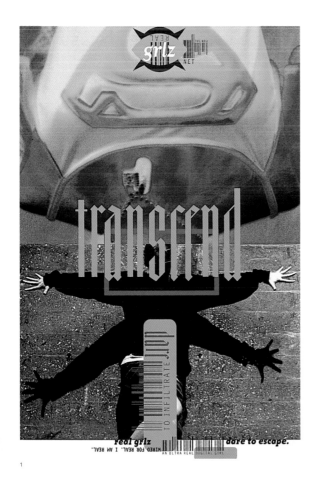

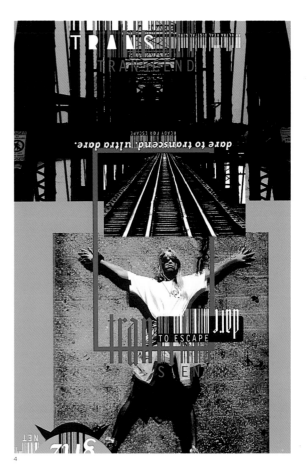

Transcend: 1. Dare to Infiltrate, 2. Dare to Decode, 3. Dare to Be., 4. Dare to Escape

USA 1996 Digital image (Magazine spreads) 雑誌 (デジタルイメージ)
CD, AD, D, P, CW: Liisa Salonen P: Sue Anne Farris CW: Elizabeth Salonen DF: Cranbrook Academy of Art Design Studio
CL: Liisa Salonen (Self-published) Typeface Design: CodeBlue by Liisa Salonen
• CodeBlue, Base, Letter Gothic
＊see p217

THEATER AAN DE HAVEN VRAAG NAAR

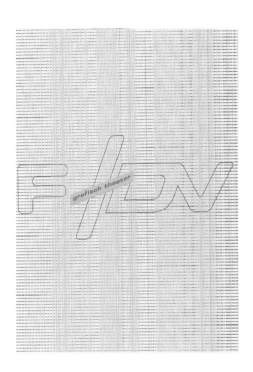

Grafisch Theater

The Netherlands 1997 Brochure ブローシャ
CD, AD, D, DF: Harmine Louwé
CL: Faydherbe / De Vringer
• Akzidenz Grotesk, Eurostile

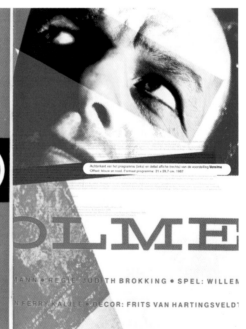

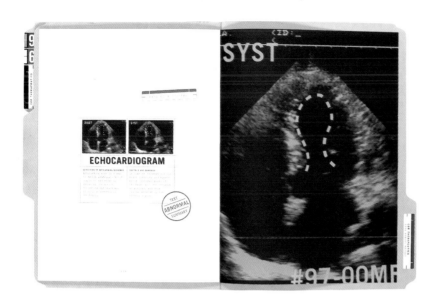

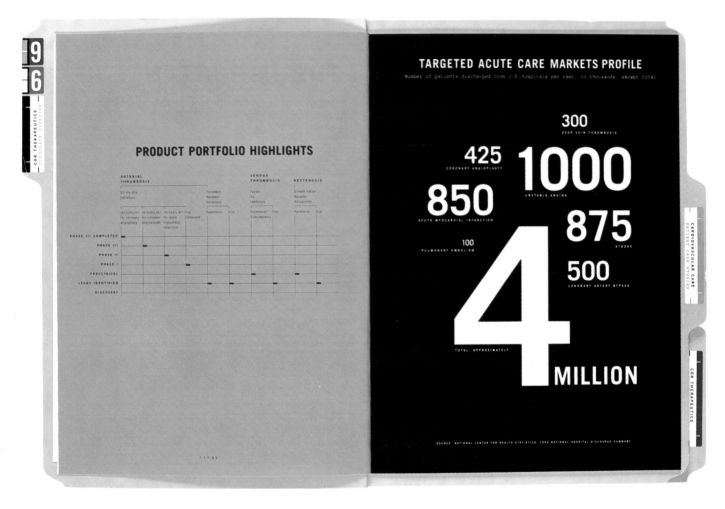

COR Therapeutics 1996 Annual Report

USA 1997 Annual report アニュアルレポート
CD, AD: Bill Cahan
D, I: Kevin Roberson
P: Keith Bardin / John Kolesa
    / Tony Stromberg
CW: Mark Bernstein / Alicia Limbora
    / Jackie Jeffries
DF: Cahan + Associates
CL: COR Therapeutics
• Trade Gothic, Courier, Orator

Fast Company Magazine

USA 1997 Magazine 雑誌
Design Direction: Pat Mitchell
AD, D: Clifford Stoltze
D: Wing Ip Ngan / Dina Radeka
I: Joe Polevy
DF: Stoltze Design
CL: Fast Company Magazine
• Bell Gothic

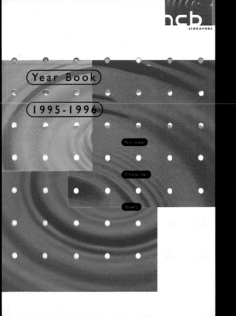

Year Book

1995-1996

National

Computer

Board

Overview

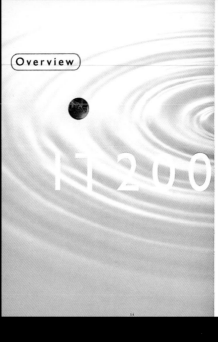

IT 2000

The 1996 World Competitiveness Report has once again placed Singapore second in the world in exploiting IT for business competitiveness. In terms of computer access, Singapore was ranked 12 in the world, and was top in Asia, with 207 computers for every 1000 Singaporeans. Singapore's internet connection of 7.74 for every 1,000 population is the highest in Asia. In another report, the 1996 Global Competitiveness Report, Singapore was ranked the second most computer-literate country in the world.

Our IT industry continued to be vibrant. Total sales of hardware, software and IT services grew by 34.3% to a record $6.7 billion last year. Export sales accounted for 51% of this total while domestic sales accounted for the remaining 49%.

FY95 saw the NCB taking significant steps to rationalise its organisation structure to better focus on delivering IT2000 capabilities to various economic sectors and the society.

From 1 April 1996, the NCB divested its system development role in the Civil Service Computerisation Programme (CSCP) to National Computer Systems Pte Ltd (NCS), to focus primarily on its IT architect and catalyst roles. A new Government Chief Information Office (GCIO) was set up in the new NCB to drive the next phase of computerisation in the Civil Service, focusing on developing and establishing Civil Service-wide IT masterplans, standards, policies and practices. The GCIO is also responsible for spearheading the integration of IT systems across ministries.

Clusters were formed within the new NCB to mirror the key economic and user sectors in Singapore. Each cluster takes a total approach in exploiting IT in the sector, addressing technology, business and IT policy issues. The clusters identify and spawn flagship applications in their

sectors, promote the development and investment of IT-related activities, and rally the industry to collectively drive IT2000 projects.

The new NCB continued to nurture the local IT industry into one of the high-growth sectors in Singapore. New incentive schemes, such as the Innovation Development Scheme (IDS) initiated by the Economic Development Board (EDB), were tapped on to encourage local companies to innovate and be more competitive. A number of promising local enterprises were identified to be nurtured into home-grown multinational corporations within the next five years.

Extending the reach of IT to the man-in-the-street remained one of the main priorities of the new NCB. Promotional and educational programmes were organised for the general population to make them better aware of IT and its applications, and to increase their IT literacy.

> *Clusters formed within the new NCB take a total approach in exploiting IT in various economic and user sectors, addressing technology, business and IT policy issues.*

Contents

The NCB logo

The new NCB logo is made up of the logotype NCB against an image of a ripple. The source of the ripple in the logo portrays the Board's role as the catalyst of Singapore's IT vision. The ever expanding ripple reflects the increasing influence of IT as it embraces all aspects of our lives - at work, at home and at play. The blue signifies authority while the orange colour suggests creativity, modernity and dynamism.

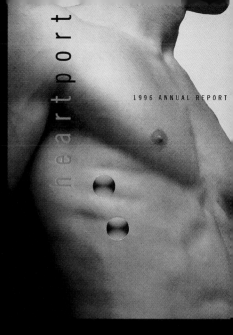

heartport

recovery periods range from four to twelve weeks following conventional open-chest heart surgery

recovery anticipated to be approximately two weeks following Port-Access™ minimally invasive cardiac surgery

patient profile: john auer

AFTER BEING DIAGNOSED WITH SEVERE TRIPLE-VESSEL CORONARY ARTERY DISEASE, JOHN AUER UNDERWENT PORT-ACCESS CORONARY ARTERY BYPASS. HE WAS ABLE TO RETURN TO RIDE HIS BELOVED RACING BICYCLE WITHIN HIS RECOVERY PERIOD FOLLOWING SURGERY AT THE NYU MEDICAL CENTER.

triple-vessel CABG

DIAGNOSIS:
MULTI-VESSEL CORONARY ARTERY DISEASE,
SEVERE LEFT ANTERIOR DESCENDING
CLAD: OBSTRUCTION,
DIAGONAL OBSTRUCTION, CIRCUMFLEX OBSTRUCTION

Father of four and master bicyclist, John Auer had a strong desire to take personal responsibility for his own health care. He had a family history of heart disease. When he felt an odd discomfort in his chest while training in December 1996, he immediately contacted his physician. A stress test, followed by an angiogram, indicated he had severe blockages on several major coronary arteries. His cardiologist wanted him to stay in the hospital and have open-chest CABG surgery immediately, but he wanted a second opinion.

Mr. Auer spent hours doing his homework. At first, he was simply seeking a qualified doctor for a second opinion about whether he needed surgery. But when he discovered information about minimally invasive heart surgery, he decided that if he needed coronary surgery, he wanted that approach. He learned from his own research that the Port-Access approach was available for multi-vessel CABG surgery. He contacted Stephen B. Colvin, M.D., chief of cardiothoracic surgery at New York University (NYU) Medical Center, who had performed the first triple-vessel Port-Access CABG operation. Dr. Colvin confirmed that Mr. Auer was a viable candidate for triple-vessel surgery with the Port-Access CABG System.

"I still got a second opinion from a cardiologist to confirm that I needed surgery," says Auer. "He was frank and told me my blockages

could be cleared with angioplasty instead of bypass surgery. But there was a 20 percent risk of restenosis (reblockage) in each of the three arteries within a year, whereas with bypass surgery, the arteries should stay clear for many years. It seemed to me that the minimally invasive surgery would not be much more massive than angioplasty, at least relative to open-chest surgery. I decided to have the minimally invasive surgery at NYU."

"When I woke up following my surgery, the surgeons were there and told me the surgery had gone very well. I had 100 percent blood flow in all three vessels."

Mr. Auer was discharged from the hospital less than four days after his surgery. He never filled his prescription for mild pain medicine. Within a week of surgery, he had resumed most normal activity, and within two weeks, he had returned to his vigorous bicycle training schedule.

"This technique wasn't even available a matter of weeks before my surgery," reflects Auer. "I feel lucky. My timing couldn't have been better."

photographed by
Jonathan
Lennard

SHOOTER

SEX
a love story
PUNK

Rage Magazine

USA 1997 Magazine 雑誌
CD, AD, D: Mike Salisbury
D: Mary Evelyn McGough / Mick Haggerty
 / Will Evans
I: Margo Chase / others
DF: Mike Salisbury Communications Inc.
CL: Rage Magazine

Argentina 1996
Magazine advertising 雑誌広告
CD: Hernan Ponce
AD, D: Marcela Augustowsky
P: Fabris / Truscello
CW: Alberto Ponte
Agency: Young & Rubicam, Argentina
CL: Produccion y Distribucion

IT'S TIME TO DRINK BEER THAT DOESN'T BELONG ON THE SAME SHELF AS BOTTLED WATER. IT'S MILLER TIME.

IT'S THAT TIME AGAIN.

IT'S TIME TO DRINK BEER IMPORTED ALL THE WAY FROM MILWAUKEE. IT'S MILLER TIME.

Miller Genuine Draft
- Sports Illustrated Insert

USA 1997 Magazine 雑誌
CD: John Boiler
AD: Jeff Williams
D: Hal Wolverton / Alicia Johnson
DF: Johnson & Wolverton
CL: Wieden & Kennedy
• Interstate-BC Miller, Interstate

Nike Olympics Campaign

USA 1996 Magazine 雑誌
CD, AD, CW: Wieden & Kennedy
CD: John Jay
AD: John Boiler
D: Hal Wolverton / Alicia Johnson
CW: Ernest Lupinacci
D, DF: Johnson & Wolverton
CL: Wieden & Kennedy / Nike, Inc.
• Franklin #2 Xtra Condensed,
  Century Old Style, Impact

USA 1997 Brochure ブローシャ
CD, P: Mike Salisbury
D: Mary Evelyn McGough
I: Doyle Harrison
DF: Mike Salisbury Communications Inc.
CL: Chris Haines-Baja Off Road Tours

Baja Off Road Tours

An honorary citizen of Ensenada, Baja California, Mexico. A legendary, award-winning factory mechanic. A fierce competitor and Baja class winner. An expert on riding in Baja and on making first-timers a first-class experience.

Chris Haines, also known in the Baja peninsula as "Señor Chris," brings not only an understanding of the expanses, terrain and challenges of Baja to his operation, but also a camaraderie with its people. Chris is no stranger to Baja; he's competed here, wrenched here and won here. He knows where the best trails are, how to get his party safely through them and how to match off-road riders with riding areas that truly suit their abilities. In short, he and his team will do all the work for you, so that you can concentrate on riding and having a good time.

Chris is no stranger to keeping things running either. With over 25 years experience as a top-level factory tuner, Chris has worked with such notable National and World Champions as Bruce Penhall, Tony DiStefano, Brian Myerscough, Darrel Schultz, Ron Lechien, Danny Laporte and Mickey Dymond. Along with helping these Speedway, Motocross and Off-Road superstars, Chris earned his own accolades along the way as a four-time A.M.A. Golden Wrench winner and six-time Motocross des Nations factory motocross tuner.

It shouldn't be surprising that Baja Off-Road Tours has been featured twice on ESPN's "Motoworld" and that they host an annual celebrity ride each spring. In his own right Chris can compete with the best too. He's garnered class wins in the Baja 1000 and Baja 500 along the way, accumulating thirteen Baja 1000 race finishes and two S.C.O.R.E. class championships. His experience in Baja benefits all of his riders. He can offer advice and tips on technique, practice and running the desert at racing speeds.

A resident of California, with bases in Southern California and Ensenada, Mexico, Chris splits his time between the two countries. Since the cooler months are the best for riding in Baja, it's not surprising that October through May are Chris' busiest months.

Design: Mike Salisbury Communications 310 300 7800

chris haines

men's journal
magazine says

Aspects of
Contemporary Photography
1995

miyuki ichikawa kyo___ ___ida takehiko goi hiro sato kunie sugiura masato seto asako na___ ___i naoya hatakeyama taiji matsue akira yoshimura

another reality

現代写真の動向

1

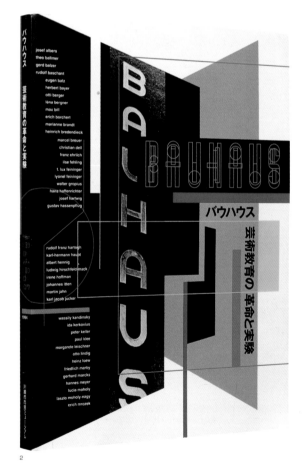

2

3

1. **Another Reality**

Japan 1995 Catalog カタログ
AD: Hitoshi Nagasawa
D: Kazutoshi Sakamoto
DF: Papier Collé S. A.
CL: Kawasaki City Museum
• Serpentine Bold Oblique, Resbaloso

2. **Bauhaus - Revolution und Experiment der Kunstausbildung**

Japan 1994 Catalog カタログ
AD: Hitoshi Nagasawa
D: Kazutoshi Sakamoto
DF: Papier Collé S.A.
CL: Kawasaki City Museum
• Original fonts

3. **Kawasaki Monument**

Japan 1994 Catalog カタログ
AD: Hitoshi Nagasawa
D: Kazutoshi Sakamoto
DF: Papier Collé S. A.
CL: Kawasaki City Museum
• Ocra, Helvetica Neue Heavy

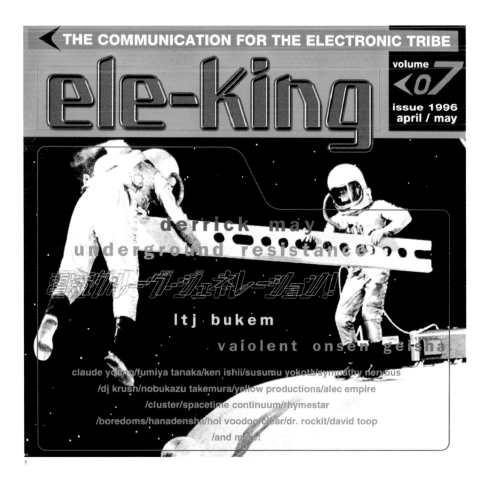

1,3. *Ele-King Vol. 7 / Vol. 12*

Japan 1996 / 1997　Magazines 雑誌
AD: Hitoshi Nagasawa
D: Kazutoshi Sakamoto
DF: Papier Collé S. A.
CL: ele-ments

2. *War in the Age of Intelligent Machines*

Japan 1997　Book cover ブックカバー
AD, D: Hiroshi Nakajima
DF: Plank
CL: ASCII

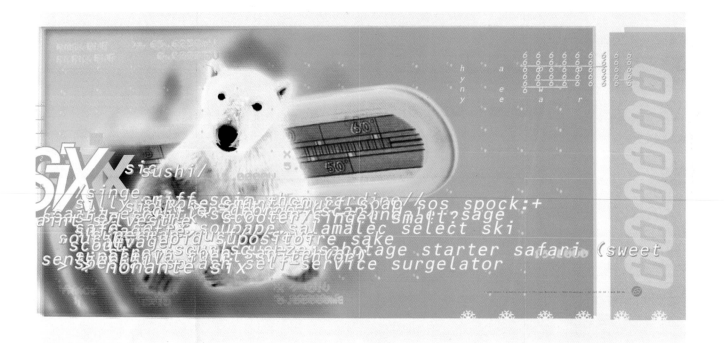

Belgium 1997
Greeting card グリーティングカード
CD, AD, D, I, CW: Nathalie Pollet
D, I: Dirk Hermans
／ Francisca Mendonça
DF, CL: Signé Lazer
• Ocrb

Air Garden

UK 1997 Flyer フライヤー
CD, AD, D: Nick Crosbie
I: Simon Clark
CL: Inflate
• Helvetica

Summer of Rainbow 97

Japan 1997 Flyers フライヤー
D: Shunsuke Otake
CL: Rainbow2000
Typeface design: Shunsuke Otake

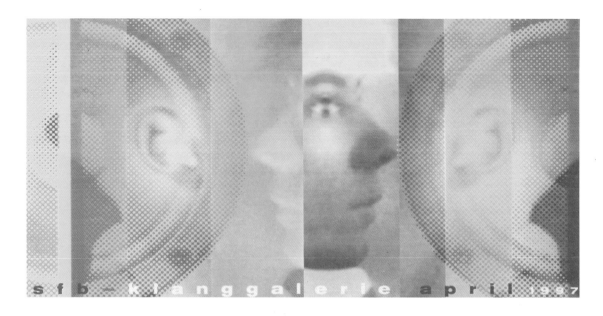

Invitations to Exhibition

Germany 1996/97 Cards カード
D: Daniela Haufe / Sophie Alex
 / Detlef Fiedler
CW, DF: Cyan
CL: Sender Freies Berlin
• Ad Grotesk

JOIN OUR TRUSTEES | FACULTY | STAFF | AND YOUR FELLOW ALUMNI

SATURDAY
APRIL

12 |4|97

ART CENTER COLLEGE OF DESIGN

European ALUMNI
REUNION

MUSEO DEI NAVIGLI
VIA S. MARCO | 40
MILAN | ITALY
RECEPTION | 19.30
DINNER | 20.30
MUSIC AND CONVERSATION | 22.30–1.00

THIS INVITATION ADMITS ONE GRADUATE AND
ONE GUEST | THERE IS NO CHARGE FOR THIS
EVENT | BUT YOU MUST MAKE A RESERVATION
BY MARCH 24 |

CONTACT THE ART CENTER ALUMNI AFFAIRS OFFICE BY PHONE
1 818 396 2305 | FAX 1 818 405 9104 | OR

to join us for an evening of
REMINISCING | NETWORKING | AND RENEWING ACQUAINTANCES ...

Art Center College of Design will be in your area soon! An admissions representative will be
available to answer your questions about portfolio requirements, financial aid, curriculum,
Art Center facilities, and visiting the campus. So put together your most recent work
and plan to meet us at one of the following Portfolio Day events.

ART CENTER COLLEGE OF DESIGN

@ national
portfolio days
1996-97

national portfolio days information

OCTOBER

St. Louis, Missouri
Washington University
School of Art, Bixby Hall
314.935.7354

Phoenix, Arizona
Doubletree Suites Hotel
800.545.ARTS

Valencia, California
California Institute of the Arts
800.545.ARTS

Kansas City, Missouri
Kansas City Art Institute
800.522.5224

Minneapolis, Minnesota
Minneapolis College of Art and Design
800.874.6223

Ann Arbor, Michigan
University of Michigan
313.763.5247

NOVEMBER

Milwaukee, Wisconsin
Milwaukee Institute of Art and Design
414.291.8070

Chicago, Illinois
School of the Art Institute of Chicago
800.232.7242

Houston, Texas
Wyndham Warwick Hotel
713.526.1991

Dallas, Texas
Fairmont Hotel
214.720.5250

New York, New York
Fashion Institute of Technology
212.760.7675

DECEMBER

Washington, D.C.
Corcoran School of Art
202.628.9484

Baltimore, Maryland
Maryland Institute College of Design
410.225.2222

JANUARY

Seattle, Washington
Cornish College of the Arts
206.726.5016

Portland, Oregon
Pacific Northwest College of Art
503.226.0462

San Francisco, California
Academy of Art College
800.544.2787

San Diego, California
Handlery Hotel and Resort
800.527.OTIS

Vancouver, British Colombia
Emily Carr Institute of Art and Design
800.832.7786

FEBRUARY

Miami, Florida
New World School of the Arts
305.237.3620

Sarasota, Florida
Ringling School of Art and Design
800.255.7695

ART CENTER COLLEGE OF DESIGN
1700 Lida Street, Pasadena, CA 91103

national portfolio days **1996-97**

get connected

• Visit our Web site: http://www.artcenter.edu/

---

1. Alumni European Reunion - Milan

USA 1997
Invitation cards インビテーションカード
CD: Stuart I. Frolick
AD: Darin Beaman
D: Carla Figueroa
DF: Art Center College of Design
　　-Design Office
CL: Art Center College of Design
• Folio Information, Snell Roundhand

2. Get Connected

USA 1996
Invitation card インビテーションカード
CD: Stuart I. Frolick
AD: Darin Beaman
D: Carla Figueroa
P: Steven A. Heller
DF: Art Center College of Design
　　-Design Office
CL: Art Center College of Design
• Univers, Rose Queen

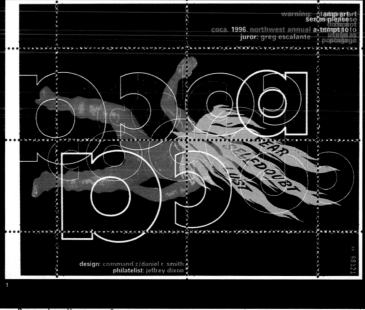

1

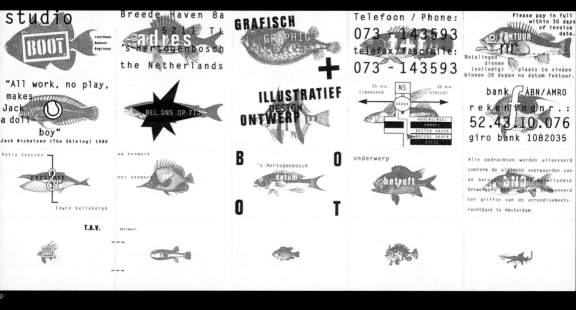

2

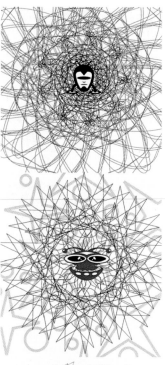

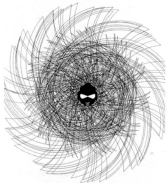

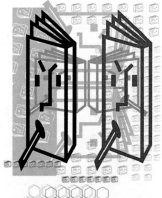

1. **Murphy Design "Hear The Buzz"**

USA 1997
Leaflet (Self promotion) リーフレット
AD, I: Mark Murphy
DF, CL: Murphy Design, Inc.
• Courier, Futura, Clique, Black Oak

2. **Gabber-G2**

Switzerland 1996
Poster ポスター/Flyer フライヤー
D: H1reber
DF: Büro Destruct
CL: Masters of Art
• Micr, Orbit

3. **Acid Boyz Strikes Back**

Switzerland 1997 Flyer フライヤー
D: H1reber
DF: Büro Destruct
CL: U1
• Büro Destruct -〈Brick〉- Font

4. **Christmas-G**

Switzerland 1996
Poster ポスター/Flyer フライヤー
D: H1reber
DF: Büro Destruct
CL: Masters of Art
• Trade Gothic

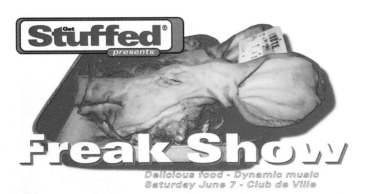

1. **Get Stuffed**

The Netherlands 1997 Flyers フライヤー
CD, AD, D: Tirso Francés
        (Dietwee Ontwerpers)
CD, AD: Arne Koefoed
        (Wink Party - artwork)
D: Dylan Fracareta
DF: Dietwee Ontwerpers
CL: Wink Party - artwork, Club de Ville
• Univers Extended

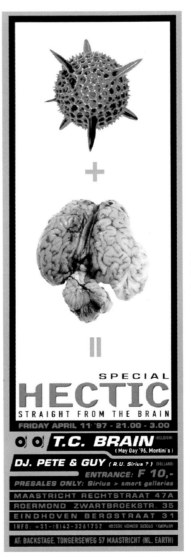

2. **Sound of the Underground, Straight from the Brain**

The Netherlands 1997 Flyers フライヤー
CD, AD, D: J.J.F.G. Borrenbergs
        / R. Verkaart
CL: Sirius, Smart Gallery

1

1. *Bar Mitzvah*

USA Leaflet リーフレット
CD: Joel Fuller
AD, D, I: Todd Houser
P: Mrs. Shusterman
CW: Frank Cunningham
DF: Pinkhaus
CL: Jared Shusterman

2.

USA 1997 Postcard ポストカード
CD, AD, D: Carlos Segura
D: Jim Marcus
DF: Segura Inc.
CL: [T-26]
• Barbera, Masoch-Dirach, Inqredients

photos>michaeldaks
representedbymajka!
mprechtandbrianben

represented by majka lamprecht & brian bennett   tel 01 212 533 3900   fax 01 212 533 4191

1. **Hi Definition Cards**

USA 1997
Promotion cards プロモーションカード
CD, AD, D: Robert Bergman-Ungar
DF: Bergman-Ungar Associates
CL: Hi Definition

2. **Micheal Dacks Promotion**

USA 1997   Brochure ブローシャ
CD, AD, D: Robert Bergman-Ungar
DF: Bergman-Ungar Associates
P, CL: Micheal Dacks

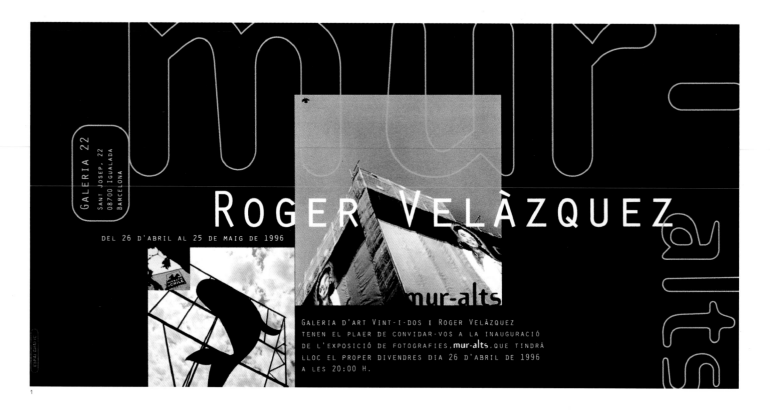

1. *Exposicio Roger Velazquez*

Spain 1996 Invitation インビテーション
CD, D: Lluis Jubert
AD, D: Ramon Enrich
P: Roger Velazquez
CW, DF: Espai Grafic
CL: Galeria 22
• Template Gothic, Orator

2. *Barna Art*

Spain 1997 Flyer フライヤー
CD, D: Lluis Jubert
AD, D, P: Ramon Enrich
CW, DF: Espai Grafic
CL: Barna Art
• Futura, Officina

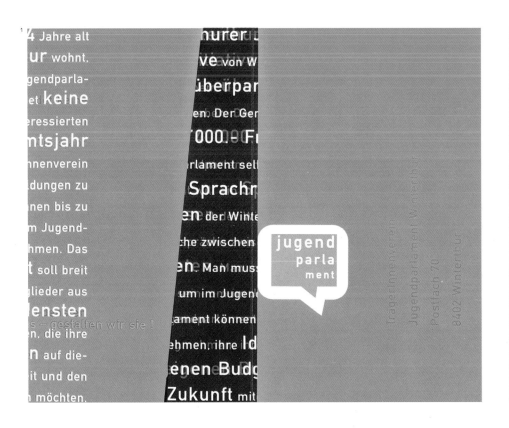

1. **Jugendparlament Winterthur**

Switzerland 1996 Pamphlet パンフレット
D: Thomas Bruggisser
DF: Grafiktraktor
CL: Stefan Fritschi
• Din Mittelschrift

2. **Bauhaus Exhibition Flyer**

Japan 1994 Flyer フライヤー
AD, D: Hitoshi Nagasawa
DF: Papier Collé S.A.
CL: Kawasaki City Museum
• Original fonts

1. *Mijn Bloed in Jouw Aderen*

The Netherlands 1995　Flyer　フライヤー
CD, AD, D: Petra Janssen
　　　　　 / Edwin Vollebergh
I, DF: Studio Boot
CL: Belgisch Toneel Amsterdam
・ Glowworm, Folio

2. *Liefde van de Zeven Poppen*

The Netherlands 1995　Flyer　フライヤー
CD, AD, D: Petra Janssen
　　　　　 / Edwin Vollebergh
I, DF: Studio Boot
CL: Belgisch Toneel Amsterdam
・ Clarendon

3.

Ireland 1996　Flyer　フライヤー
D: Peter Maybury

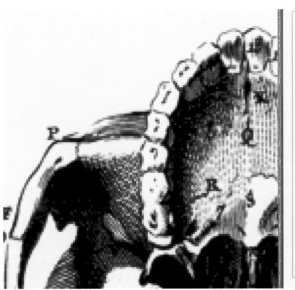

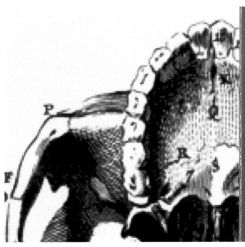

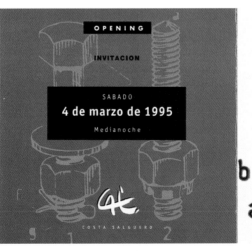

Reopening of Caix

Argentina 1996 Flyer フライヤー
CD, AD, D: Santiago Felippelli
P: Martin Sigal
I: Alejandro Melguizo
CW: Gonzalo Loper Marti
DF: Bridger Conway Ag
CL: Caix
• Meta, Mix

1

2

3

4

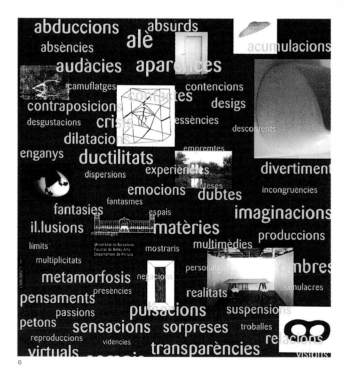

1,2,3. Promotional Cards for
New York Fashion Show

Canada 1996
Promotional cards プロモーションカード
CD, AD, D: Noël Nanton
P: Ed Chin
DF: Typotherapy + Design
CL: Anne Hung Fashion Designs Inc.
• Bell Gothic, Active, C.O.W, Helvetica

4. Journées Pédagogiques

Spain 1997 Brochure ブローシャ
CD, D: Lluis Jubert
AD, D: Ramon Enrich
CW, DF: Espai Grafic
CL: Universitat Autonoma de Barcelona
• Scala Sans

5. Fira Primavera

Spain 1995 Pamphlet パンフレット
CD, D: Lluis Jubert
AD, D: Ramon Enrich
P: Ramon Pallarés
CW, DF: Espai Grafic
CL: Foment de Fires i Mercats
• Univers Condensed

6. Triptic Pintura

Spain 1997 Pamphlet パンフレット
CD, D: Lluis Jubert
AD, D: Ramon Enrich
CW, DF: Espai Grafic
CL: Universitat de Barcelona
• Barmeno

185

Trace (urban, visual terrorism)

Greece 1996 Promotional cards プロモーションカード
CD: Apostolos Rizos (1,2) / Tasos Efremidis (3,5) / Dimitris Mitsiopoulos (4)
AD: Dimitris Mitsiopoulos(1,3,5) / Tasos Efremidis (2) / Apostolos Rizos (4)
D: Tasos Efremidis (1,4) / Dimitris Mitsiopoulos (2) / Apostolos Rizos (3,5)
DF: alterVision CL: Alternation

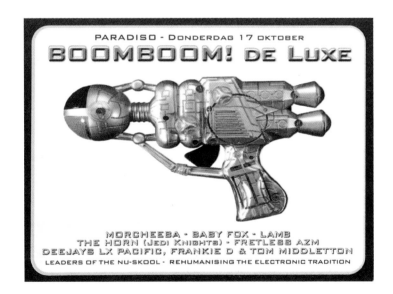

BoomBoom! de Ville / BoomBoom! de Luxe

The Netherlands 1996 Flyers フライヤー
CD, AD, D: Tirso Francés (Dietwee Ontwerpers)
CD, AD: Arne Koefoed (Wink Party - artwork)
D: Ron Faas   DF: Dietwee Ontwerpers
CL: Wink Party - artwork, Club de Ville, West-Pacific, Paradiso

SUNDAY FEBRUARI 11
SPACE FUNK

SUNDAY MARCH 10
FREEDOM

SUNDAY NOVEMBER 3
SUBMERGE

SUNDAY AUGUST 4
Midsummer-Special
Peace, love & ice-cream

WILD STYLE
SUNDAY DECEMBER 10

Amazing stuff
Peace, love & ice-cream
sunday september 1

SUNDAY JULY 7
REFUNKED!

Hardbop

The Netherlands 1996 Flyers フライヤー
CD, AD, D: Tirso Francés
(Dietwee Ontwerpers)
CD, AD: Arne Koefoed
(Wink Party - artwork)
D: Ron Faas / Harmen liemburg
 / Erik Hoogendorp / Michiel de Vreede
 / Alex Slagter
DF: Dietwee Ontwerpers
CL: Wink Party - artwork, AXL

1

2

3

4

5

6

1. **Energy**
2. **Sol For Your Soul**

Yugoslavia 1996 Flyers フライヤー
CD: Jovanovic Slobodan (2)
AD: Dragisa Čubranovic (1)
D: Aleksandar Perduh (1) / Jovanovic Slobodan (2)
I: Aleksandar Perduh (1)
CW: Integra (1) / Jovanovic Slobodan (2)
DF: Trans:East:Design
CL: Integra Productions (1) / JCPS-Bonlavoro (2)

3. **Trace (urban, visual terrorism no. 2)**

Greece 1996
Promotional card プロモーションカード
CD: Apostolos Rizos
AD: Tasos Efremidis
D: Dimitris Mitsiopoulos
DF: alterVision
CL: Alternation

4. **Trace (urban, visual terrorism no. 1)**

Greece 1996
Promotional card プロモーションカード
CD: Tasos Efremidis
AD: Apostolos Rizos
D: Dimitris Mitsiopoulos
DF: alterVision
CL: Alternation

5,6. **Taurus**

Yugoslavia 1996 Flyer フライヤー
AD: Jovanovic Slobodan
D: Aleksandar Perduh
CW: Integra
DF: Trans:East:Design
CL: Integra Productions

1

Alexandre Godeau
director

arkham s.a./n.v.
rue du collégestraat, 27
1050-Bruxelles/Brussel

T: 32 2 644 37 38
F: 32 2 646 24 61
alexandre@arkham.be
http://www.arkham.be

@rkham

2

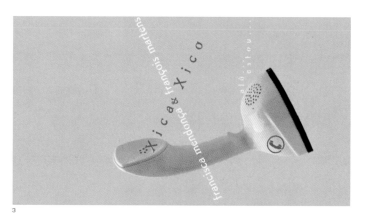

3

4

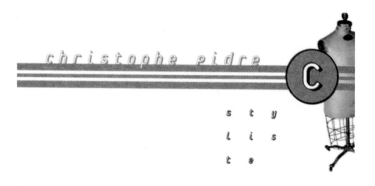

5

6

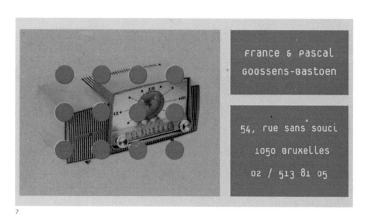

7

Belgium 1997
Business cards 名刺/Postcard ポストカード (8)
CD: Nathalie Pollet (2,8)
AD: Nathalie Pollet (ex.3,8)
 / Francisca Mendonça (3)
D: Nathalie Pollet (ex.3)
 / Francisca Mendonça (3)
I: Nathalie Pollet (ex.2,3)
DF: Signé Lazer
CL: Nathalie Pollet and Friends (ex.2,3,8)
 / Arkham (2)
 / Francisca Mendonça (3)
 / Signé Lazer (8)
• Ariston, Platelet,
 Matrix Script Inline (ex.2,3,8), Din (2,8)

signé lazer

8

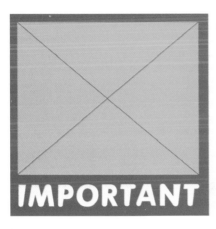

all products designed by inflate. design rights reserved.
5 old street. london. ec1 v 9hl. england.

this product captures the essence of the inflate spirit:
to invent fun functional and affordable designs that can be enjoyed by
everyone. →

if this product proves defective. or if you want to find out more about
inflate please call 0+44 (0171) 250 0706. fax 0+44 (0171) 250 0311.

blow hard and enjoy

IMPORTANT

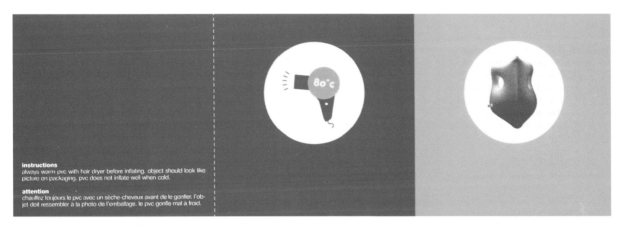

instructions
always warm pvc with hair dryer before inflating. object should look like
picture on packaging. pvc does not inflate well when cold.

attention
chauffez toujours le pvc avec un sèche-cheveux avant de le gonfler. l'ob-
jet doit ressembler à la photo de l'emballage. le pvc gonfle mal à froid.

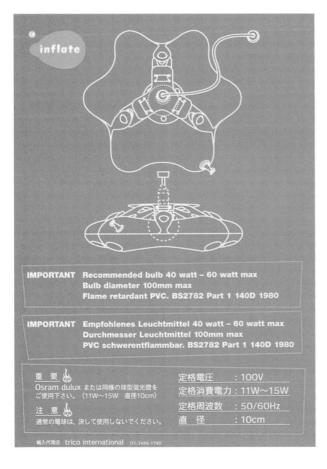

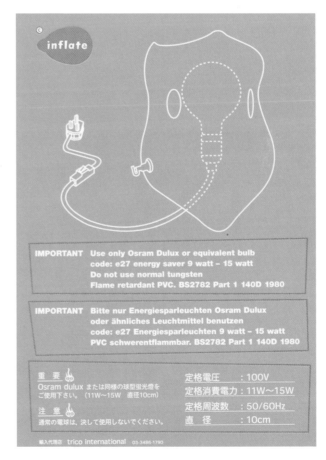

Light Instructions /
Inflating Instructions

UK 1997 Inserts 説明書
AD: Nick Crosbie
D, I: Simon Clark / Belinda Moore
CL: Inflate
• Helvetica

Quadrant
communicatie

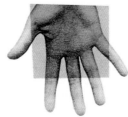

Quadrant
communicatie

1.

The Netherlands 1997　Business cards 名刺
D: Ron Faas / Tirso Francés
　/ Annelies Dollekamp / Tanja Kumpermondt
DF: Dietwee Ontwerpers
CL: Quadrant Communicatie
• VAG Rounded, Glassgow

2. *Oracle Stationery*

USA 1996　Stationery ステーショナリー
CD, AD: Bill Cahan
D, I: Bob Dinetz
DF: Cahan + Associates
CL: Oracle
• Caslon, Futura

Teresa Galí i Izard
Via Augusta, 24, 1er, 2a
08006 Barcelona

Tel. 93 - 217 15 88
Fax 93 - 415 61 73

paisatgista

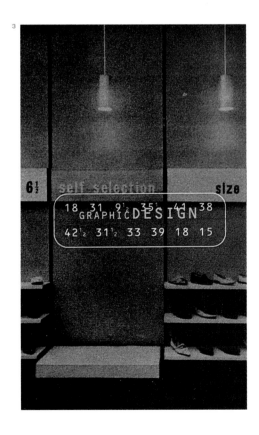

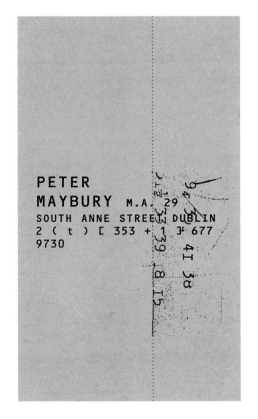

1.

Germany 1996
Promotional cards プロモーションカード
D: Daniela Haufe
DF, CL: Cyan

2. **Teresa Gali Cards**

Spain 1997 Cards カード
CD, D: Lluis Jubert
AD, D: Ramon Enrich
P: Teresa Gali
CW, DF: Espai Grafic
CL: Teresa Gali
• Hand lettering, Scala Sans

3.

Ireland 1996 Business cards 名刺
D, P: Peter Maybury
CL: Peter Maybury
• Ocrb, Din Mittleschrift

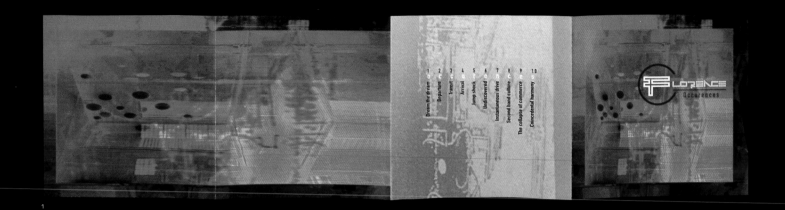

1	Trip to the Inner Spaces	Traveller	6.11	(M. v.d. Heuvel / P. v.d. Pas)	
2	So why is it fresh?	The Deep	5.51	(M. Hendrikx)	
3	Underground never stops	R. de la...Gauthier	6.22	(R. de la Gauthier / Th. Vogel)	Publ. de la...Musique
4	Taking over	Dis' ko 3000	7.29	(P. Gijselaars / E. Overdijk)	Polygram Music Publ.
5	Tweeker	Exxit	7.25	(P. Gijselaars / E. Overdijk)	Polygram Music Publ.
6	Funk me up	Dis' ko 3000	6.18	(P. Gijselaars / E. Overdijk)	Polygram Music Publ.
7	Voicebox	Kosmik Indian	5.51	(E. Overdijk)	Polygram Music Publ.
8	Behaviour	Traveller	5.48	(M. v.d. Heuvel / P. v.d. Pas)	
9	Trump 'n' Bass	Funckarma	6.07	(R. Funckard)	
10	Zoom	Android	8.11	(R. Funckard)	
11	Random	The Deep	6.03	(M. Hendrikx)	
	Artwork	Stoere Binken Design	3.21	(J. Borrenbergs / R. Verkaart)	

1. **Florence, Occurences**

The Netherlands 1997 CD
CD, AD, D: J.J.F.G.Borrenbergs
    / R.Verkaart
CL: New Electronica

2. **SOS, Sounds of the Underground**

The Netherlands 1997 CD
CD, AD, D: J.J.F.G.Borrenbergs
    / R.Verkaart
CL: Sirius, Smart Gallery

3. **Terrace, Konnekt**

The Netherlands 1996 CD
CD, AD, D, P: J.J.F.G.Borrenbergs
    / R.Verkaart
CL: Eevo Lute Muzique

1. *Anon CD*

USA 1995 CD package
AD, D: Clifford Stoltze
I: Cynthia von Buhler / Polly Becker
/ Glenn Wurz / James Kraus
/ James Gallagher / Jordin Isip
/ Calef Brown / Mick Aarestrup
/ John Weber / Vicky Rabinowicz
/ Dmitry Gurevich / Juliette Borda
/ Tracy Mitchell / Nancy Jo Haselbacher
/ The Sisters Carrozza / Christine Red
/ David Pohl / Melinda Beck
/ Patrick Cunningham / David Miller
/ Susan Farrington / Eric White
/ Bina Altera / Cristina Casanas
/ Mark S. Fisher / Peter K. Wyckoff
/ Carl Dunn / Nataliya Gurshman
DF: Stoltze Design
CL: Castle von Buhler

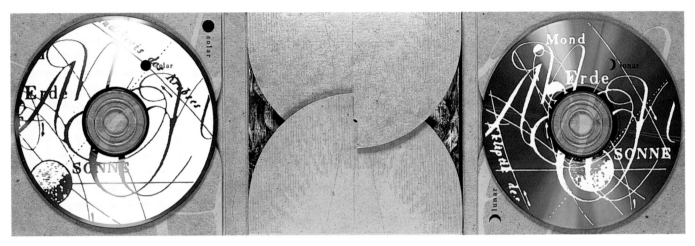

2. *Las Blacanblus*

Argentina CD
CD, AD, D: Marcela Augustowsky
P: Fabris / Truscello
DF: Augustowsky Design
CL: BMG
Calligraphy: Marcela Augustowsky

197

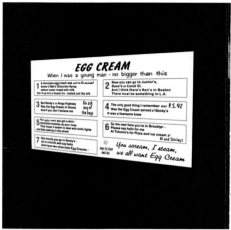

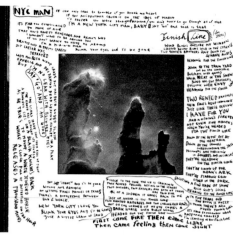

1. Lou Reed "Set the Twilight Reeling"

USA 1996 CD
CD, AD, D: Stefan Sagmeister
D: Veronica Oh
P: Timothy Greenfield Sanders
I: Tony Fitzpatrick
CW: Lou Reed
DF: Sagmeister Inc.
CL: Warner Bros.
• Hand type, Spartan, News Gothic

2. Aerosmith "Nine Lives"

USA 1997 CD
CD, AD, D: Stefan Sagmeister
D: Hjalti Karlson
P: F. Scott Schafer
I: Hungry Dog Studios
CW: Aerosmith & AL
Photo Art Direction: Chris Austopchuk
                    / Gail Anderson
DF: Sagmeister Inc.
CL: Sony / Columbia
• Mrs. Eaves, Calligraphy, Hand type,
Bembo Sabon, etc.

198

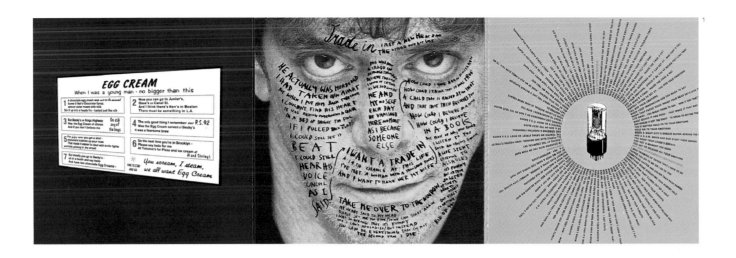

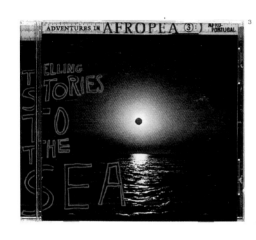

3. *Telling Stories to the Sea*

USA 1996 CD
CD, AD, D: Stefan Sagmeister
D: Veronica Oh
P: Tom Schierlitz
I: Indigo Arts
CW: David Byrne / Morton Marks
DF: Sagmeister Inc.
CL: Lauka Bop / David Byrne
• Hand type, Trade Gothic,
  Bembo Sabon, Times, Frutiger

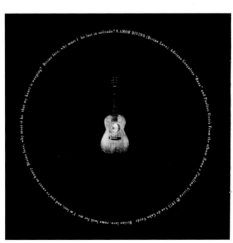

199

1. *Two Thirds, 'Ease The Pressure' remix*

UK 1994 CD
CD, AD, D, I: Paul West
CD, AD, D: Paula Benson
P: Tim Platt
DF: Form
CL: Epic Records
• Ocrb

2. *Two Thirds, 'I Want The World'*

UK 1994 CD
CD, AD, D, I: Paul West
CD, AD, D: Paula Benson
P: Lawrence Watson
DF: Form
CL: Epic Records
• Ocrb

tin tin out ™

Dance With Me featuring Tony Hadley

Written by Edwards/Stokes/Hadley except 4 - written by
Edwards/Stokes. Produced by Tin Tin Out. 5 - Remix & additional
production by the Sharp Boys for Sharp Productions. Published
by Copyright Control/Notting Hill Music (UK) Ltd./Biostream
Music. 4 - Published by Copyright Control/Notting Hill Music
(UK) Ltd. The copyright in this recording is owned by Virgin
Records Ltd. ℗ 1997 Virgin Records Ltd. © 1997 Virgin Records
Ltd. This label copy information is the subject of copyright
protection. All Rights Reserved. ℗ 1997 Virgin Records Ltd.
Printed in the UK. 7243 8 94215 2 1 PM 515 VCRD17 LC 3098
Design: **Form** (www.form.uk.com).

1. Dance With Me 03.32
(Radio Edit)
2. Dance With Me 03.58
(Extended Single Mix)
3. Dance With Me 07.52
(Tin Tin Out Mix)
4. Trance With Me 06.54
5. Dance With Me 09.17
(Sharp Mad House Remix)

Dance With Me
is taken from
**Adventures in
Tin Tin Out Land**

Also available in the
tin tin out series,
All I Wanna Do

UFO photographed
north of Kelsey Bay,
Vancouver Island, British
Columbia, Canada,
October 1981

UFO photographed near
Albuquerque, New Mexico,
USA, 1986 June 1953

tin tin out ™

All I Wanna Do

The new single from their
Adventures in Tin Tin Out Land
27.01.97

Adventures in
Tin Tin Out Land

1

2

tin tin out ™
Adventures in Tin Tin Out Land

3

4

1. **Tin Tin Out, 'Dance With Me'**

UK 1997 CD cover
CD, AD, D: Paul West
CD, AD: Paula Benson
D: Malcolm Buick
P: Fortean Times Picture Library
DF: Form
CL: Virgin / VC Records
• Luvbug, Helvetica Neue

2. **Tin Tin Out, 'All I Wanna Do'**

UK 1996 Mini poster ミニポスター
CD, AD, D: Paul West / Paula Benson
D: Malcolm Buick
P: Fortean Times Picture Library
DF: Form
CL: Virgin Records
• Luvbug, Helvetica Neue

3,4. **Tin Tin Out, 'Adventures...'**

UK 1996 CD cover
CD, AD, D: Paul West
CD, AD: Paula Benson
D: Malcolm Buick
P: Fortean Times Picture Library
DF: Form
CL: Virgin / VC Records
• Luvbug, Helvetica Neue

1

2

3

4

5

6. *Rare Groove 1 & 2 Mixed Tape Insert*

Canada 1996
Tape Inserts カセットテープ
CD, AD, D: Noel Nanton
P: John Klich (Rare Groove 2)
DF: Typotherapy + Design
CL: Vibes'n Stuff 89.5 FM
• Frutiger, Helvetica

7. *Sweet Revenge,*
Ryuichi Sakamoto

USA 1997 CD
CD, AD, D: Robert Bergman-Ungar
P: Jean Baptiste Mondino
DF: Bergman-Ungar Associates
CL: Gut / For Life
• Helvetica

1. J-Pac 'She Loves Me'

UK 1996 Mini poster ミニポスター
CD, AD, D: Paul West
CD, AD: Paula Benson
D: Lisa Smith
DF: Form
CL: East West Records
• Bull (in-house font)

2. The Gigantic Recording Corporation Proudly Presents

USA 1994 CD cover
AD, D, I: Robynne Raye
DF: Modern Dog
CL: Giant Records
• Spumoni, Clarendon

3. Everything But The Girl - 'Walking Wounded'

UK 1996 LP sleeve
CD: EBTG
CD, AD, D: Paul West / Paula Benson
P: Marcelo Krasilcic
DF: Form
CL: Virgin Records
• Handel Gothic, Meta

4. Everything But The Girl - 'Before Today'

UK 1996 CD cover
CD: EBTG
CD, AD, D: Paula Benson / Paul West
P: Jeuren Teller
DF: Form
CL: Virgin Records
• Handel Gothic, Meta

5. The Professional School of Techno Vol. 2

Japan 1994 CD
AD: Hitoshi Nagasawa
D: Kazutoshi Sakamoto
DF: Papier Collé S.A.
CL: Sony Records
• Original fonts

1. *Shift Record Sleeve*

UK 1997   Record sleeve レコード
CD, AD, D: Rian Hughes
DF: Device
CL: Shift Recordings
Typeface Design: Rian Hughes
• Outlander, Foonky

2. *Record Sleeve for Metropolitan Records*

UK   Record sleeve レコード
CD, AD, D, P: Rian Hughes
DF: Device
CL: Metropolitan Records
• Univers

3. *Transient Single Bag*

UK 1997   Record sleeves レコード
CD, AD, D: Rian Hughes
DF: Device
CL: Transient
Typeface design: Device
• Amorpheus, Regulator

4. *Transient 3*

UK 1997   Record sleeves レコード
CD, AD, D, P: Rian Hughes
DF: Device
CL: Transient
Typeface design: Device
• Amorpheus

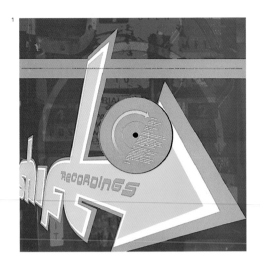 

1. *Pell Mell LP*

USA 1996   Record jackets レコード
AD, D, P: Clifford Stoltze
D: Robert Beerman
DF: Stoltze Design
CL: David Geffen Company
• Interstate, Platelet

2. *Artie Phartie T-Shirt*
/ Professor Love T-Shirt

UK 1996   T-Shirts Tシャツ
CD, AD, D, I, CW: Rian Hughes
DF: Device
CL: Million Dollar
Typeface design: Device
• Knob Cheese, Contour

XXX Waxtins Display

USA 1996 Packaging パッケージ
CD, AD, D, I: Carlos Segura
I: Tony Klassen
DF: Segura, Inc.
CL: XXX
• Amplifier, Cyberotica

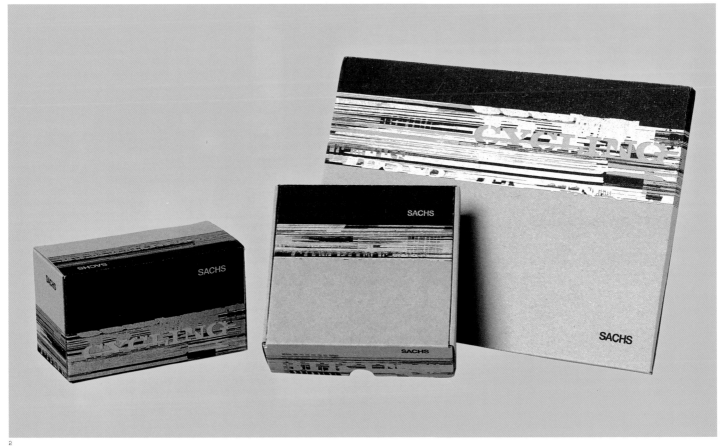

1. *ADP Packaging*

Germany 1996 Packaging パッケージ
CD, AD, D, I: Ruediger Goetz
DF: Simon & Goetz
CL: ADP Engineering GmbH
• Trade Gothic

2. *Sachs Packaging*

Germany 1996 Packaging パッケージ
CD, AD, D, I: Ruediger Goetz
P: Rui Camillo
I: Chris Rehberger
DF: Simon & Goetz
CL: Fichtel & Sachs AG
• Helvetica

1. **J-Pac Shop Door Sign**

UK 1996
Shop door sign ドアサイン
CD, AD, D: Paul West
CD, AD: Paula Benson
DF: Form
CL: East West Records
• Bull, Stemplate Gothic (in-house font)

2. **Barbie Goes Vegas**

Switzerland 1997
Poster ポスター/Flyer フライヤー
D: Lopetz
DF: Büro Destruct
CL: Öff Öff Productions
• Moonbase Alpha, Ocr B

3. **Grotesque Seven Nine**

USA 1996 Poster ポスター
CD, AD, D, P, CW: Liisa Salonen
CW: David Berlow / Thomas Hansard
DF: Cranbrook Academy of Art Design Studio
CL: Liisa Salonen (Self-published)
• Grotesque Seven Nine

1. Apollo Ale & Lager Packaging

USA 1996 Packaging パッケージ
CD, AD: Bill Cahan
D, I: Kevin Roberson
CW: Stefanie Marlis
DF: Cahan + Associates
CL: Boisset USA
• Futura

2. Alcatraz Ale Packaging

USA 1996 Packaging パッケージ
CD, AD: Bill Cahan
D: Sharrie Brooks
DF: Cahan + Associates
CL: Boisset USA
• Univers, Officiana, Din Neuzeit Grotesk

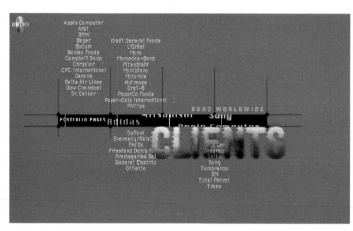

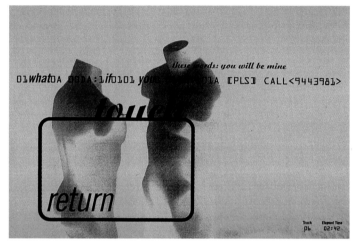

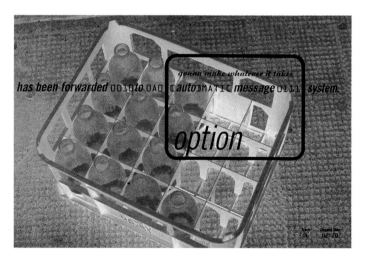

1. *BBDO Worldwide Web Site*

USA 1996 Web site ホームページ
CD: Jennifer Boyd / BBDO
Concept Manager: Somi Kim
AD: Whitney Lowe
D: Beth Elliott / Jens Gehlhaar
/ Ken Olling / Scott Fishkind
DF: ReVerb
CL: BBDO / West
• Customized fonts including
Laika (Jens Gehlhaar)

2. *Min / Max*

USA 1996 Self-published book 書籍
CD, AD, D, P, CW: Liisa Salonen
CW: Jean Baudrillard / REM
DF: Cranbrook Academy of Art Design Studio
CL: Liisa Salonen (Self-published)
• Trade Gothic, Peignot, Ariston, Ocra Ocrb

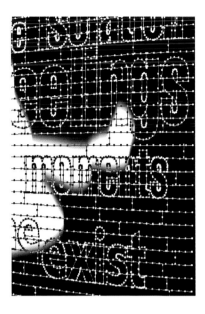

1. Exist

Italy 1996 Slide Installation スライド
CD, AD, D, P, I, CW: Justin Greenleaf
DF: N. A. C.
CL: Costume National
• Helvetica, Outline

*2. How can we find something that will not
be on the level of a hallucination?*

Italy 1997
Video for shop window display ビデオ
CD, AD, D, CW: Justin Greenleaf
DF: N. A. C.
CL: Costume National
• Helvetica, Clarendon, Shelley

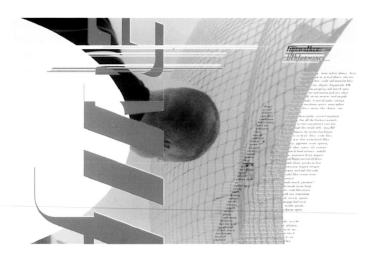

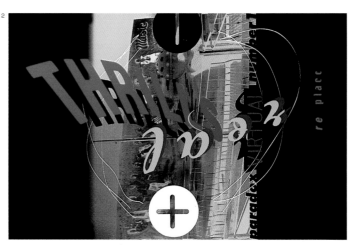

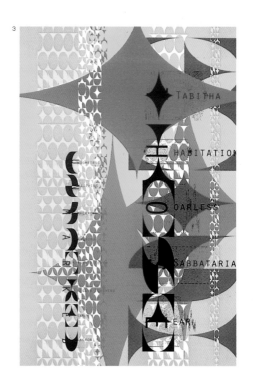

1. *UltraGirl*

USA 1997 Magazine spreads 雑誌
CD, AD, D, I, CW: Liisa Salonen
 / Summer Powell
P: Shayne Christiansen / Shuichi Murakami
DF: Cranbrook Academy of Art
CL: Marvin Jarrett
• UltraGirl Bold, Peignot, Typattern
*→see p217

2. *Real Thrills, Real Dogs*

USA 1996 Digital Image デジタルイメージ
CD, AD, D, P, I, CW: Liisa Salonen
DF: Cranbrook Academy of Art Design Studio
CL: Liisa Salonen (Self-published)
• Vernacular Type, Trade Gothic, Sucker, But

3. *Tags for Those Unmarked*

USA 1997
Experimental typeface design
タイプフェイスデザイン
CD, AD, D, I, CW: Summer Powell
DF: Cranbrook Academy of Art Design Studio
CL: Summer Powell (Self-published)
Typeface Design: Typattern by Summer Powell
• Typattern, Orator
*→see p217

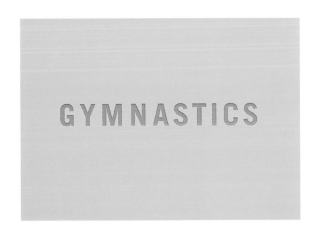
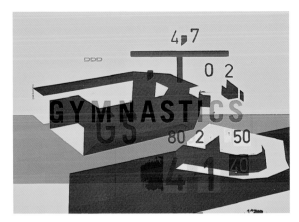

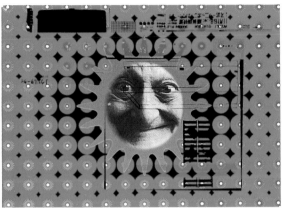

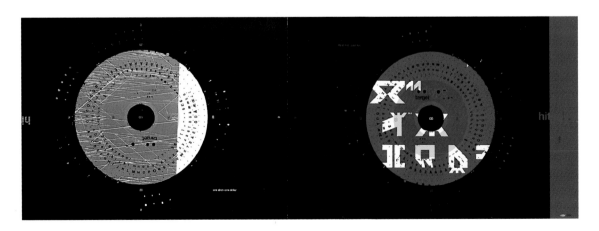

GYMNASTICS

Switzerland 1996 Catalog カタログ
D, I: Lopetz / H1 / MBrunner / Pedä
DF: Büro Destruct
CL: Self promotion
• Cover: Trade Gothic,
  Inside: Büro Destruct Fonts,
    Helvetica Neue

1. Sports Final

USA 1997 Video ビデオ
CD, AD, D: James A. Houff
CL: WDIV / TV
• Axion, Bank

2. It Is

USA 1997 Video ビデオ
CD, AD, D: James A. Houff
CL: WDIV / TV
• Monospace

1. *Think Sharp*

USA 1996 Poster ポスター
CD, AD, D, P, I, CW: Jim Poore Ⅳ
DF: Poore House Design
CL: Personal
• Variex, Raygun, Handcut

2. *Situation*

Japan 1996 Publication 書籍
AD: Hiroshi Nakajima
DF: Plank
CL: Sakuhin Sha

'Image of Eighties' Remix: Twentieth Century Type   Japan 1997   Artwork アートワーク   D, I: Naomi Enami   Cl: Lewis Blackwell   • Chicago

P.23—1.

聖人と呼ばれながら、最後には殺人者となったメインキャラクターのメタファーとして、O.J.シンプソンの写真が使われている。引用文は「いい試合だ。幸運をもとめての闘い」。

The picture of O.J.Simpson is used as a metaphor for the main character, who is considered a kind of saint, but finally turns out to be a murderer. The quote says: "It's a nice play, the strive for luck."

P.68—1,2.

中国の筆文字と伝統的な書の道具の使用が、静の文化に到達しようとする、デザイナーと漢字とのセンチメンタルな絆を現わしている。

Chinese calligraphy and traditional writing tools are used to show the sentimental ties between design creators and Chinese characters in the attainment of cultural   tranquility.

P.69—2.

1997年は牛年であると同時に、香港にとっては重大な年でもある。歴史的な返還の前後には、解決されなければならない様々な問題があり、中国政府と英国政府の間での対話が不可欠となる。中国語の熟語『牛頭搭馬嘴』の反意語がこのポスターのタイトルである。対話こそが問題解決の始まりである。

1997 is the Year of the Ox, and an important year for Hong Kong There are many problems to solve before and after the historic handover, and communication is essential between the Chinese and British governments. An antonym of a Chinese idiom was used as the title of this poster, and suggests that communication is the beginning of problem solving.

P.80 / P.81

コードブルーは、ゴシック文字（大文字）とバーコード（小文字）を上下に組み合わせたタイプフェイスである。バーコードを読む、あるいは両方を同時に読むことによって、異なる2種類のメッセージを得ることができる。

In the typeface CodeBlue, the Gothic face is the upper case and the barcode is the lower case. You can get 2 different messages from the text by reading only the lower case, or by reading the upper and lower cases together.

P.152

観客に、動き、反射、感触などの様々な知覚対象に気付かせることによって、新たな発見と心に残る何かが生まれる。行間に隠されたメッセージやサブテキストは、内緒話を囁くがごとく、読者を魅了する。ひとつのドアが開かれたとき、読者は次のドアを探すものである。『ヘンリー』では、私は物語の内側と外側、感情を読み取るという体験、話す声の大きさと速さに興味があった。半透明のページをめくると、暗い森の中をわずかな光に導かれるかのように、状況の手がかりが現われる。二番目の声がページの裏側から現われ、内側から浮き上がり、サブテキスト、つまり、表面には現れないストーリーの内側からの声を聞かせるのである。

By attempting to make viewers aware of various perceptions - moving images, reflection, texture - a new awareness and enticement can result. Hidden messages or subtexts intrigue the reader in the same way a whispered rumor does. As one door opens, the reader searches for more. In my book Henry, I was interested in the inside and outside of narrative and the experience of reading the emotion, volume and speed of the spoken voice. The turning of the translucent pages reveals clues about the environment as you are led through the dark woods. A second voice appears on the back side of the pages, embossed from the inside, exposing a subtext - the inner voice which relates the under current of the story.

P.212—1,3.

タイパターンは、パターンのモジュールに、音のフォントと言葉のフォントが調和した、可読性のあるタイプフェイスである。

Typatern is a semi-legible typeface of modular patterns with a corresponding font of sound and of words.

Index of Submitters

New Typographics 2
ニュータイポグラフィックス　2

Jacket Design
cyan berlin

Art Director
Yutaka Ichimura

Designer
Tomoko Sekine

Editor
Tomoe Nakazawa

Photographer
Kuniharu Fujimoto

Translators
Sue Herbert
Douglas Allsopp
Setsuko Noguchi

Coordinator
Maya Kishida

Typesetter
Yutaka Hasegawa

Publisher
Shingo Miyoshi

1997年11月30日　初版第1刷発行

定価（本体15,500円＋税）

発行所　ピエ・ブックス
〒170 東京都豊島区駒込4-14-6-301
編集　Tel:03-3949-5010 Fax:03-3949-5650
営業　Tel:03-3940-8302 Fax:03-3576-7361
e-mail: piebooks@bekkoame.or.jp

©1997 P·I·E Books

Printed in Singapore

ISBN4-89444-056-3 C3070　¥15500E

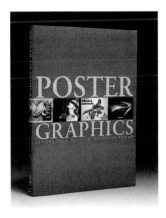

POSTER GRAPHICS Vol. 2
好評！業種別世界のポスター集大成、第2弾
Pages: 256（192 in color）￥16,505＋Tax
700 posters from the top creators in Japan and abroad are showcased in this book - classified by business. This invaluable reference makes it easy to compare design trends among various industries and corporations.

CALENDAR GRAPHICS Vol. 2
好評カレンダー・デザイン集の決定版、第2弾
Pages: 224（192 in Color）￥15,534＋Tax
The second volume of our popular "Calendar Graphics" series features designs from about 250 1994 and 1995 calendars from around the world. A special collection that includes mass market as well as exclusive corporate PR calendars.

BROCHURE & PAMPHLET COLLECTION Vol. 4
好評！業種別カタログ・コレクション、第4弾
Pages: 224（Full Color）￥15,534＋Tax
The fourth volume in our popular "Brochure & Pamphlet" series. Twelve types of businesses are represented through artwork that really sells. This book conveys a sense of what's happening right now in the catalog design scene. A must for all creators.

BROCHURE DESIGN FORUM Vol. 3
世界の最新カタログ・コレクション、第3弾
Pages: 224（Full Color）￥15,534＋Tax
A special edition of our "Brochure & Pamphlet Collection" featuring 250 choice pieces that represent 70 types of businesses and are classified by business for handy reference. A compendium of the design scene at a glance.

COMPANY BROCHURE COLLECTION
業種別（会社・学校・施設）案内グラフィックス
Pages: 224（192 in Color）￥15,534＋Tax
A special selection of brochures and catalogs ranging from admission manuals for colleges and universities, to amusement facility and hotel guidebooks, to corporate and organization profiles. The entries are classified by industry for easy reference.

COMPANY BROCHURE COLLECTION Vol. 2
業種別会社案内グラフィックス、第2弾！
Pages: 224（Full Color）￥15,534＋Tax
Showing imaginative layouts that present information clearly in a limited space, and design that effectively enhances corporate identity, this volume will prove to be an essential source book for graphic design work of the future.

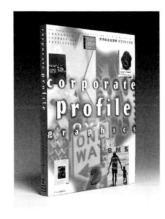

CORPORATE PROFILE GRAPHICS Vol. 2
世界の会社案内グラフィックス、第2弾
Pages: 224（Full Color）￥15,534＋Tax
An extensive collection of company brochures, annual reports, school facility guides and organization pamphlets. Brochures are fully detailed from cover to inner pages, illustrating clearly the importance of cohesiveness and flow. An essential catalog design reference volume.

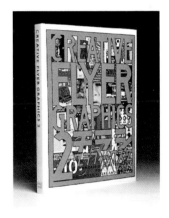

CREATIVE FLYER GRAPHICS Vol. 2
世界のフライヤーデザイン傑作集
Pages: 224（Full Color）￥15,534＋Tax
A pack of some 600 flyers and leaflets incorporating information from a variety of events including exhibitions, movies, plays, concerts, live entertainment and club events, as well as foods, cosmetics, electrical merchandise and travel packages.

EVENT FLYER GRAPHICS
世界のイベントフライヤー・コレクション
Pages: 224（Full Color）￥15,534＋Tax
Here's a special selection focusing on flyers promoting events. This upbeat selection covers a wide range of music events, as well as movies, exhibitions and the performing arts.

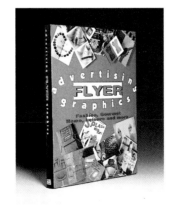

ADVERTISING FLYER GRAPHICS
衣・食・住・遊の商品チラシ特集
Pages: 224（Full Color）￥15,534＋Tax
The eye-catching flyers selected for this new collection represent a broad spectrum of businesses, and are presented in a loose classification covering four essential modern lifestyle themes: fashion, dining, home and leisure.

TRAVEL & LEISURE GRAPHICS
ホテル＆旅行案内グラフィックス
Pages: 224（Full Color）￥15,534＋Tax
A giant collection of some 400 pamphlets, posters and direct mailings exclusively created for hotels, inns, resort tours and amusement facilities.

SPECIAL EVENT GRAPHICS
世界のイベント・グラフィックス
Pages: 224（192 in Color）￥15,534＋Tax
A showcase for event graphics, introducing leaflets for exhibitions, fashion shows, all sorts of sales promotional campaigns, posters, premiums and actual installation scenes from events around the world. An invaluable and inspirational resource book, unique in the world of graphic publishing.

1, 2 & 3 COLOR GRAPHICS Vol. 2
1・2・3色グラフィックス、第2弾
Pages: 224 (Full Color)　¥15,534＋Tax
Even more ambitious in scale than the first volume, this second collection of graphics displays the unique talents of graphic designers who work with limited colors. An essential reference guide to effective, low-cost designing.

1 & 2 COLOR GRAPHICS
1色＆2色デザインの大特集
Pages: 224 (Full Color)　¥15,534＋Tax
Powerful design achieved by restricting colors, unusual combinations of colors that grab the attention, enhanced stylishness of script... all artwork featured in this worldwide collection makes a dramatic visual impact. A useful book, too, for exploring the possibilities of low-cost design.

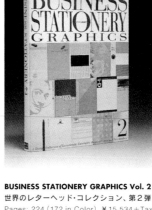

BUSINESS STATIONERY GRAPHICS Vol. 2
世界のレターヘッド・コレクション、第2弾
Pages: 224 (172 in Color)　¥15,534＋Tax
The second volume in our popular "Business Stationery Graphics" series. This publication focuses on letterheads, envelopes and business cards, all classified by business. This collection will serve artists and business people well.

NEW BUSINESS CARD GRAPHICS
最新版！ビジネスカード・グラフィックス
Pages: 224 (Full Color)　¥15,534＋Tax
A selection of 900 samples representing the works of top designers worldwide. Covering the broadest spectrum of business cards, it ranges from the trendiest to the most classy and includes highly original examples along the way.

BUSINESS PUBLICATION GRAPHICS
業種別企業PR誌・フリーペーパーの集大成！
Pages: 224 (Full Color)　¥15,534＋Tax
This comprehensive graphic book introduces business publications created for a variety of business needs, including promotions from boutiques and department stores, exclusive clubs, local communities, and company newsletters.

BUSINESS PUBLICATION GRAPHICS Vol. 2
大好評！業種別PR誌の集大成、第2弾
Pages: 224 (Full Color)　¥15,534＋Tax
One volume offering more than 150 samples of regularly published PR and other informative magazines, covering different business sectors from fashion labels to non-profit organizations. This overviews the current trends in PR magazine design aimed at attracting the attention of a specific readership in commercial activities.

POSTCARD GRAPHICS Vol. 4
世界の業種別ポストカード・コレクション
Pages: 224 (192 in Color)　¥15,534＋Tax
Our popular "Postcard Graphics" series has been revamped for "Postcard Graphics Vol. 4." This first volume of the new version showcases approximately 1,000 pieces ranging from direct mailers to private greeting cards, selected from the best around the world.

SEASONAL CAMPAIGN GRAPHICS
デパート・ショップのキャンペーン広告特集
Pages: 224 (Full Color)　¥15,534＋Tax
A spirited collection of quality graphics for sales campaigns planned around the four seasons, Christmas, St. Valentine's Day and the Japanese gift-giving seasons, as well as for store openings, anniversaries, and similar events.

SHOPPING BAG GRAPHICS
世界の最新ショッピングバッグ・デザイン集
Pages: 224 (Full Color)　¥15,534＋Tax
Over 500 samples of the latest and best of the world's shopping bag designs from a wide range of retail businesses! This volume features a selection of shopping bags originating in Tokyo, NY, LA, London, Paris, Milan, and other major cities worldwide, presented here in a useful business classification.

ILLUSTRATION IN GRAPHICS
イラストレーションを使った広告特集
Pages: 224 (Full Color)　¥15,534＋Tax
Delivering the message faster than photos and more accurately than words, illustration never fails to stir the imagination. This superb selection presents some 600 first-class illustrations for advertising from across the business spectrum and for editorial designs.

PRESENTATION GRAPHICS
制作の現場 プレゼンテーション・グラフィックス
Pages: 224 (Full Color)　¥15,500＋Tax
31 designers from 8 countries explain the production side of the creative process. Here are idea sketches, comps, presentations, and final works, all with explanatory notes by the designer. This is a unique volume that peeks behind the scenes of the creator's world.

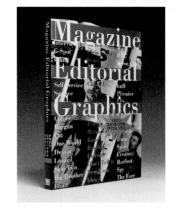

MAGAZINE EDITORIAL GRAPHICS
世界のエディトリアル＆カバーデザイン特集
Pages: 224 (Full Color)　¥15,500＋Tax
A special collection of editorial and cover designs. Stylish and sophisticated, 79 topical books from 9 countries were selected. Including top creators' graphic works, innovative fashion photography, and the latest typography, this is a true creator's bible for the New Age.

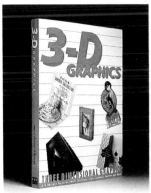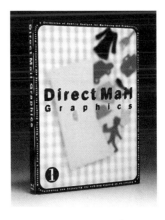

3-D GRAPHICS
3Dグラフィックスの大百科
Pages: 224 (192 in Color) ￥15,534＋Tax
350 works that demonstrate some of the finest examples of 3-D graphic methods, including DMs, catalogs, posters, POPs and more. The volume is a virtual encyclopedia of 3-D graphics.

**PROMOTIONAL GREETING CARDS
ADVERTISING GREETING CARDS Vol. 4
(English Title)**
世界の案内状＆ダイレクトメール集大成
Pages: 224 (Full Color) ￥15,534＋Tax
A total of 500 examples of cards from designers around the world. A whole spectrum of stylish and inspirational cards, classified by function for easy reference.

DIRECT MAIL GRAPHICS Vol. 1
衣・食・住のセールスDM特集
Pages: 224 (Full Color) ￥15,534＋Tax
The long-awaited design collection featuring direct mailers that have outstanding sales impact and quality design. 350 of the best pieces, classified into 100 business categories. A veritable textbook of current direct marketing design.

DIRECT MAIL GRAPHICS Vol. 2
好評！衣・食・住のセールスDM特集！第2弾
Pages: 224 (Full Color) ￥15,534＋Tax
The second volume in our extremely popular 'Direct Mail Graphics' series features a whole range of direct mailers for various purposes; from commercial announcements to seasonal greetings. Classfied by industry.

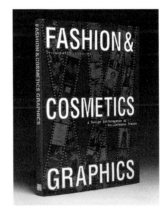

SUCCESSFUL DIRECT MAIL DESIGN
セールス効果の高いDMデザイン集！
Pages: 224 (Full Color) ￥15,500＋Tax
This collection features product flyers, service guides, shop opening and sale announcements, school and industrial promotions, and a variety of event invitations. A valuable book that captures the essence of today's direct marketing design.

The Paris Collections / INVITATION CARDS
パリ・コレクションの招待状グラフィックス
Pages: 176 (Full Color) ￥13,396＋Tax
This book features 400 announcements for and invitations to the Paris Collections, produced by the world's top names in fashion over the past 10 years. A treasure trove of ideas and pure fun to browse through.

FASHION & COSMETICS GRAPHICS
ファッション＆コスメティック・グラフィックス
Pages: 208 (Full Color) ￥15,534＋Tax
A collection of promotional graphics from around the world produced for apparel, accessory and cosmetic brands at the avantgarde of the fashion industry. 40 brands featured in this book point the way toward future trends in advertising.

THE TOKYO TYPEDIRECTORS CLUB ANNUAL 1995-96
TDC 年鑑95-96
Pages: 250 (Full Color) ￥16,505＋Tax
A follow-up publication to Japan's only international graphic deisgn competition. Featuring 650 typographic artworks selected by THE TOKYO TYPEDIRECTORS CLUB, this book provides a window to the latest typographic design concepts worldwide.

The Production Index ARTIFILE Vol. 5
最新版プロダクション・クリエーター年鑑
Pages: 224 (Full Color) ￥12,136＋Tax
ARTIFILE 5 features artwork from a total of 100 top Japanese production companies and designers, along with company data and messages from the creators. An invaluable information source for anyone who needs to keep up with the latest developments in the graphic scene.

CARTOON CHARACTER COLLECTION
5500種のキャラクターデザイン大百科
Pages: 480 (B&W) ￥3,600＋Tax
A collection of illustrations from successful character artists. People, animals, plants, food, vehicles, landscapes, sports, seasons... Nearly 5,500 works are presented, conveniently categorized. A collection full of ideas sure to come in handy when designing greeting cards and illustrations.

CATALOGUE AND PAMPHLET COLLECTION / Soft Jacket
業種別商品カタログ特集／ソフトカバー
Pages: 224 (Full Color) ￥3,689＋Tax
A collection of the world's most outstanding brochures, catalogs and leaflets classified by industry such as fashion, restaurants, music, interiors and sporting goods. Presenting each piece in detail from cover to inside pages. This title is an indispensable sourcebook for all graphic designers and CI professionals.

SPORTS GRAPHICS / Soft Jacket
世界のスポーツグッズ・コレクション／ソフトカバー
Pages: 224 (192 in Color) ￥3,689＋Tax
A Collection of 1,000 bold sporting goods graphic works from all over the world. A wide variety of goods are shown, including uniforms, bags, shoes, and other gear. Covers all sorts of sports: basketball, skiing, surfing, and many, many more.

THE P·I·E COLLECTION

LABELS AND TAGS COLLECTION Vol. 1 / Soft Jacket
ラベル＆タグ・コレクション／ソフトカバー
Pages: 224 (192 in Color) ￥3,689＋Tax
Nowhere is brand recognition more important than in Japan. Here is a collection of 1,600 labels and tags from Japan's 450 top fashion names with page after page of women's and men's clothing and sportswear designs.

FASHION INSIGNIA COLLECTION / Soft Jacket
ワッペン・コレクション／ソフトカバー
Pages: 224 (Full Color) ￥3,689＋Tax
Over 300 designs were scrutinized for this collection of 1000 outstanding emblems and embroidered motifs. Visually exciting, they make innovative use of materials and compliment the fashions with which they are worn.

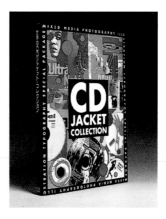

CD JACKET COLLECTION / Soft Jacket
世界のCDジャケット・コレクション／ソフトカバー
Pages: 224 (192 in Color) ￥3,689＋Tax
Featuring 700 of the world's most imaginative CD and LP covers from all musical genres, this is a must-have book for all design and music professionals.

POSTCARD COLLECTION Vol. 2 / Soft Jacket
好評 ポストカード・コレクション、第2弾／ソフトカバー
Pages: 230 (Full Color) ￥3,689＋Tax
Welcome to the colorful world of postcards, with 1200 postcards created by artists from all over the world classified according to the business of the client.

POSTCARD COLLECTION / Soft Jacket
世界のポストカード・コレクション／ソフトカバー
Pages: 240 (Full Color) ￥3,689＋Tax
Postcards from top Japanese designers, fashion brands, and famous shops. This book shows how designers, using beautiful photos and fun illustrations, pack a lot of creativity into a postcard's limited space.

DIAGRAM COLLECTION
世界のダイアグラム・デザイン集大成
Pages: 224 (192 in Color) ￥3,700＋Tax
Graphs, charts, maps, architectural diagrams and plans, product and scientific illustrations. Almost 400 diagrams selected from designs sent to us by some of the world's most talented creators. This invaluable volume shows the many possibilities of diagram design.

WORLD BUSINESS CARD COLLECTION
世界の名刺コレクション Vol. 2
Pages: 224 (192 in Color) ￥3,700＋Tax
From personal and business cards, bursting with individuality, to colorfully creative shop cards, we introduce nearly 1,000 of the best. Limited in size, these designs mix fun and cleverness, and will impress and delight you with their originality.

カタログ・新刊のご案内について
総合カタログ、新刊案内をご希望の方は、はさみ込みのアンケートはがきをご返送いただくか、90円切手同封の上、ピエ・ブックス宛お申し込み下さい。

CATALOGUES ET INFORMATIONS SUR LES NOUVELLES PUBLICATIONS
Si vous désirez recevoir un exemplaire gratuit de notre catalogue général ou des détails sur nos nouvelles publications, veuillez compléter la carte réponse incluse et nous la retourner par courrierou par fax.

CATALOGS and INFORMATION ON NEW PUBLICATIONS
If you would like to receive a free copy of our general catalog or details of our new publications, please fill out the enclosed postcard and return it to us by mail or fax.

CATALOGE und INFORMATIONEN ÜBER NEUE TITLE
Wenn Sie unseren Gesamtkatalog oder Detailinformationen über unsere neuen Titel wünschen, fullen Sie bitte die beigefügte Postkarte aus und schicken Sie sie uns per Post oder Fax.

ピエ・ブックス
〒170 東京都豊島区駒込 4-14-6-301
TEL: 03-3940-8302 FAX: 03-3576-7361

P·I·E BOOKS
#301, 4-14-6, Komagome, Toshima-ku, Tokyo 170 JAPAN
TEL: 03-3940-8302 FAX: 03-3576-7361